Kevin & Bri

May the words upon these pages be a blessing to you.

Judy

Home 810.638.7260
Cell 810.813.3472

TRUTH SHALL SET YOU FREE

A Journey from Legalism and OCD to Salvation

JUDITH EVANS

WestBow Press books may be ordered through booksellers or by contacting:

WestBow Press
A Division of Thomas Nelson & Zondervan
1663 Liberty Drive
Bloomington, IN 47403
www.westbowpress.com
844-714-3454

ISBN: 978-1-6642-5446-6 (sc)
ISBN: 978-1-6642-5444-2 (hc)
ISBN: 978-1-6642-5445-9 (e)

Library of Congress Control Number: 2022901846

Print information available on the last page.

WestBow Press rev. date: 04/28/2022

Truth Shall Set You Free[1]

CONTENTS

ACKNOWLEDGMENTS

I would like to acknowledge

- my heavenly Father, who loves me immensely (Romans 8:15);
- His precious Son, Jesus, my Lord and Savior, my Redeemer, and my Brother;
- Holy Spirit, who counsels me and speaks truth to me (John 16:13);
- and all of my family, biological and blood-bought, and friends who have loved me in the midst of all my struggles.

INTRODUCTION

I am not a medical professional. This story is not told in thorough medical terms; nor is it meant to be. From a layperson's perspective, obsessive-compulsive disorder, abbreviated as OCD, is something that has gone awry in your life, evidenced by a relentless attack against your mind, followed by incessant unhealthy thinking, culminating in goofy, if not more-goofy-than-the-thoughts actions.

These thoughts and actions occur in a cycle that seems to repeat itself over and over and over again. After having done something goofy in response to an unhealthy thought, you find yourself wishing that you hadn't reacted the way that you did. But somewhere later, you find yourself responding in a similar way again, just in a different setting with different circumstances. OCD is a terrible intruder that you want to go away; you want both the goofy thoughts and actions to stop, but for whatever reasons, you have a hard time getting rid of them.

Sometimes, these cycles are not limited to one specific arena. You might master one area of conflict just to find the OCD crop up in another. Or you might be dealing with OCD in a number of areas at the same time, and you realize that you are able to categorize them into their specific domains.

Others don't understand why you say and do the things you do; what's worse is that even *you* don't understand your own behavior. As a result of unhealthy thinking and living, the person with

OCD experiences consequent guilt, pain, rejection, confusion, and erosion of self-esteem. My experience of living with OCD was one of lingering pain. The degree of seriousness to which obsessive-compulsive disorder affected my life also had residual impact upon the lives of those around me. I am *so* much better than what I was years ago, but I still have a ways to go.

A story comes to my recollection. Years ago, Pastor Robert Vaughn told of an elephant that was tied to a stake. When he was released from the stake, he neglected to walk away from it. I believe that God has freed me from OCD, but it is a matter of me walking in the freedom with which I have been blessed. I don't do it faultlessly, but I am way, way better than what I was!

It has involved me receiving truth, being transformed in my thinking, applying that new thinking, breaking habits—some of which existed for years—letting go, trusting God, staying in God's Word, and resisting the devil and unhealthy living.

I have experienced a grieving in my life pertaining to the OCD, because there comes a time when you realize what you have lost. Much of my childhood lacked the carefree spirit that usually accompanies childhood. I was much too serious and worried. My best friend in high school once told me that if I didn't have something to worry about I wouldn't be normal. I realize my behavior affected my relationships with people in a negative way, particularly those with my children and first husband, who has passed on. Even though it was not intentional, you realize that damage was done and that you cannot go back and do it over. You're sad for what you've lost and sad for what you've done.

A number of factors might have played into the development of OCD in my life, but there is one catalyst that I suspect played a prominent role for me, starting at an early age. It was a knowing of the existence of hell, knowing the possibility of me going there, and, more important, *not knowing* God's plan of salvation for me through the shed blood of His precious Son, Jesus Christ.

Years ago, as an adult, I was lying in bed, and I heard the

words "Truth shall set you free" or "Truth shall make you free" (or something similar). I actually *heard* words. The words may not have been audible to the *physical* ear; maybe the Holy Spirit was making them audible to my spirit man. I don't know for sure how to explain it, but somehow, I *heard* words.

At first, I didn't know *what* that truth was that was going to set me free. At that time, I don't know if I even *knew* of the term *OCD*. In retrospect, I now know that that "truth" entailed the Word of God, Jesus Himself, and revealed truth regarding myself. Truth is truth. Whatever the truth was, that I was ignorant of, that I needed to correct faulty thinking, *that* was the truth I needed. Sometimes, we suffer because of the fact that we don't know pertinent information (Hosea 4:6).

What I am about to tell in the following pages of this book is how God delivered me from the bondage that I was in. I will tell about the personal God that I have come to know and the wonderful truths that He has revealed to me in His Word. It is my prayer that as you read the pages of this book, that God Himself, by the power of His Holy Spirit, will illumine your mind and heart so that you, too, can experience the freedom that I have found.

CHAPTER 1

My Life with OCD

I grew up as one of the older children in a large family with many brothers and sisters. Also being a twin, I became too reliant on having a companion by my side. I am an extrovert but, at times, would be content to stay within my comfort zone and sometimes lacked the confidence or assertiveness to venture into new territory on my own.

We attended church faithfully, and I went to parochial school for most of my elementary and junior high years. It was during that time that my formal religious education began.

I was taught the existence of hell and still believe in that existence. However, I did not fully understand God's plan of salvation; I developed an unhealthy fear of going to hell. So I did the best that I could to avoid going there, and for me, that involved getting into legalism big-time. I didn't know the term *legalism* at the time, but that's what it was. I latched on to all kinds of law—the Ten Commandments, church law, self-imposed law, and so on. It developed to the point that I was constantly watching myself to make sure that I was being good and not doing bad. I call it *covering the bases.*

As time progressed, I developed the habit of being too concerned about whether or not I had committed a mortal sin. This became a pretty big issue for me. What if I wasn't judging myself correctly? I was conscious of having a way to get to church to go to confession, and I didn't want to be asking about it too often. My unhealthy conscience and the need for a way to get to confession posed a dilemma. Sometimes, I would say the recommended prayers more than the specified number of times in case I hadn't paid attention to the words well enough when I had said them the first time. In time, my problem began to be recognizable.

I became preoccupied with the question of whether I had given full attention to the main elements of the Mass. Had I meant the words that were spoken during these times?

Sometimes, while numerous people were going forward to receive Communion, I would stay in my pew. I was conscious of all these other people going past me as I sat in my pew, but I didn't want to take the chance of sinning. What if I hadn't properly met the requirements for receiving Communion?

I did lots of babysitting through the years. Even in the course of babysitting, I had a mental checklist that I would go through to see if there was anything I needed to tell the parent when he or she got home. Examples would be if anything happened to the kids or if anything happened to the home or belongings.

I don't remember how old I was when the following incident occurred. Before I went home from a particular babysitting job, I had accumulated a pile of towels on top of the hamper. In my mind, it was a matter of cleanliness. I had washed my hands and then wondered, what if my hands weren't completely clean and what if I got something on the towel? So I would rewash my hands and get a clean towel to the point that I ended up with a pile of towels by the time I was done. I knew that this wasn't normal. Although obsessive hand washing wasn't a big problem for me as a young girl, I did deal with it more as an adult.

While still young, I thought it a sin to be angry. I didn't want to argue, which was good, but I carried it to an extreme—sometimes I would say nothing. This was not good for me relationally, let alone my own emotional well-being. In time, I learned that what I was doing wasn't good. As I began to open up, things improved for me.

I took driver's training at the age of fifteen. I did very well on the bookwork. Whoever scored highest on the bookwork was in the first car to drive. I ended up being in the first car but would rather have been in the last because I was afraid to drive. Although I hadn't had much experience driving anything—a tractor, snowmobile, lawnmower, and so on—a lack of driving experience was not the only factor in my problem. At the time, I did not perceive as much of a connection between the fear of driving and my other psychological/emotional problems as I do now.

Because I was so intense in my driving skills, the driver's ed teacher would purposely tell me to roll down my window or do something with the radio in order to divert my attention a little bit. My fear of driving did have its humorous side. The town I lived in was so small that it didn't even have a yellow blinking light; needless to say, the traffic was not bad at all. When it came time for me to turn a corner, I would say, "Oh, no-o-o!" Upon getting my driver's license at age sixteen, I wasn't eager to drive; I would *make* myself take the car someplace. Now I am much more relaxed driving than I was in my high school days but not as relaxed as some others are.

I carried responsibility to an extreme. Not only was I scrupulous in examining my *own* thoughts, words, and actions, but because I was *so* sin-conscious and self-conscious, I crossed another line and policed *others'* actions to the extent that I thought they affected me. This was not primarily for the sake of judging others but out of the concern that their action could result in a sin for *me*. I was taking on the role of the world's policeman, and that was not meant to be.

I would wonder if my class paper was graded correctly. Was this supposed to have been marked wrong even though it wasn't? I didn't want to get a grade that I didn't deserve.

I would pay attention to the accuracy of another's speaking and wonder if I should say something in addition or as a correction.

Or if someone was speaking badly of another person, I would be concerned if I should speak up in that person's defense and if I neglected to do so, that it might be sin on my part. I knew about slander, and I did not want to be involved in wrongfully slandering another person.

As an adult especially, I was too careful of checking prices of grocery store items. What if someone had incorrectly priced a particular item, and I did not end up paying the correct amount?

I was aware of sins of omission as well as sins of commission. Some of the aforementioned issues have their place, but I went overboard. Once while riding as a passenger, I saw something lying on the roadside. Even though the vehicle I was riding in had nothing to do with it being there, I turned back to look.

Growing up, I was a high-caliber student. I was a Brownie and Junior Girl Scout and took 4-H sewing and knitting. I accompanied on the piano for the high school music department. During my first three years of high school, I was very busy with school, homework, cheerleading, debate, forensics, and dating—not necessarily every activity every year. By the time my senior year came around, I cut back; I didn't want to be so busy.

In dealing with overconscientiousness, my speech was affected. I developed the habit of using such expressions as "I'm not sure, but …" "I think," "maybe," and "It was something like …" I probably sounded so unsure of myself, yet I am an intelligent person. I was my high school class salutatorian. I was so conscious of not wanting to tell a lie. What if I didn't remember the facts precisely? By using such expressions of speech, I was covering myself, so I thought, and also setting up a cushion to fall back on. That way, if later I questioned the accuracy of something I had said, I could rely on the fact that I had expressed doubt in my original statement.

It got to where I was mentally rehashing conversations in my head to assure myself that I hadn't told a lie or said something that I shouldn't have. This was a horrible habit. Since none of us are perfect, I would often find a problem in the conversations I had. Was I accurate? Did he understand what I was trying to say? Did they take it the wrong way? Did I say something I wasn't supposed to, and what if they in turn told it to someone else? Had I said anything that would ruin someone's reputation? Did I neglect to say something that I should have? There were endless options for error.

I also developed a habit of repeating myself. This not only helped, so I thought, with clarity if someone didn't seem to be getting what I was trying to say but, at times, might have also been an unhealthy way of confirming to myself that I had said something that I felt obligated to say. I was so full of self-doubt, backtracking and questioning how I handled situations. By repeating my words enough times, I was putting into place an assurance to address any questions that arose in my mind during the conversation and after the fact.

On the surface, there was a lot of good and a certain appearance of normalcy about me, but underneath, there was definitely something wrong, and I knew it. I didn't know fully what to do about it. It got to where I had dealt with it for so long that I learned to handle it the best that I could, whether in an unhealthy or healthy manner. At times, I was applying Band-Aids instead of getting to the root of the problem and fully addressing the situation. At some point, I became aware that other people washed their hands too often, but I don't recall knowing about OCD.

Eventually, the issue of mortal sin diminished in its importance in my life, not that it was completely gone—just diminished in its prior relevance. Some of the release of tension in this area was probably connected with my ability to drive, so I was able to go to confession whenever I sensed the need to do so.

Another reason might have been rationalization, and this could be rationalization for good or bad. I could rationalize goofy thoughts away, and I could rationalize an excuse for wrong behavior. Even though there were occasions in which I went to the extreme in attempting to do right, there were other times in which I definitely sinned.

As an adult, I would continue a conversation of time past by correcting what I had said, explaining, and apologizing (another bad habit); many times, the apology was not necessary. Once as a kid, I was lying in bed at night before going to sleep, and I called out a blanket apology to whoever would hear. It was not an apology for anything specific; otherwise, I probably would have addressed a particular person, but instead, it was an apology to *whomever* to cover *whatever* just in case.

Legalism followed me into adulthood. I married at the age of twenty. Prior to marriage, I inquired if I had met the requirements; I was concerned in part specifically regarding church law.

My husband had no denominational religious affiliation and for the most part did not go to church except for special occasions pertaining to family or friends. While we were yet newlyweds, there was an incident where I was upset to the point of tears regarding me going to confession. Here, my husband was trying to comfort me. It's ironic that he would be the one who would in time give me a Bible as a gift.

Time passed, and I became a mother. I was now a full-time homemaker and stay-at-home mom, both of which I had wanted. Eventually, I went through a period of questioning and would read my Bible looking for answers.

My husband and I were with a couple of our friends one evening. The gentleman used to work with my husband in sales but had become a Baptist minister, and his wife was sitting in the backseat of a car with me.

She said, "Judy, let's just say that you die, and you're at the pearly gates of heaven, and Saint Peter wants to know why he should let you in. What are you going to say?"

I said such things as "I'm a good person. I go to church. I ..." I caught myself. I said, "That's not it, is it?"

It was like someone had turned the light on! The true message of salvation was getting through to me. Things were coming together. I was finally getting it. The emphasis was being taken off of *me* and put on to the work that *Jesus* did on my behalf. It was through Jesus having died on the cross that I would have my salvation. I was so excited with my newfound insight.

As I came to understand more fully about God's plan for salvation, it was like a tremendous weight being lifted off of my shoulders. A Bible quotation from Ephesians 2:8–9 speaks of this truth: "For by grace you have been saved through faith; and that not of yourselves, *it is* the gift of God; not as a result of works, that no one should boast."

How liberating these words were to me! I had the verses displayed on the mirror above my kitchen sink for a long time. The words brought comfort to me and gave me truth that I needed in order to be set free from the weight of bondage to legalism that I had been in. It took the pressure off of *me*. I didn't have to be so conscious of what *I* did and what *I* didn't do.

Although I was being set free from messed-up thinking, I still had a ways to go. I was still having problems. I often would call my girlfriend back, in response to a telephone conversation that we had just had, because of a need that I felt to say something.

I was around thirty-three to thirty-five years old when I started counseling with the pastor of the church I was attending. After a length of time, he discerned that he wasn't able to give me the help that I needed. That was disturbing to me, as if it were a bad reflection on me, although he did not present it that way. It was more of a matter of how *I* was processing it.

Thus, I started professional counseling. Even in the process of trying to get professional help, I would wrestle with my words. Nothing was mentioned to me about OCD.

It was also around this time that the Holy Spirit led me into the baptism in the Holy Spirit as spoken of in Acts 2, along with blessing me with the gift of speaking in tongues. God was bringing me into more fullness of His Holy Spirit. Through another Christian, God gave me some very encouraging words: "I brought you to this church to feel love by the people and to have some healing in your emotions and healing in your overconscientiousness … I have healed you of overconscientiousness. Now walk in it … You are set free of all weights that would beset you. Weights are ills, sicknesses, problems, circumstances. Whom the Lord has set free is free indeed."

It was sometime after this that I became aware of the term "OCD" and sought professional counseling once again. It's kind of sad that it took that long for a clearer understanding of what I had been dealing with for years to be revealed to me, but according to material that I have read, the medical profession did not know years ago what it presently knows concerning OCD. In fact, it might have been to my benefit that I did not get more professional help earlier on in life because of what was *not* known about OCD at that time.

It has taken me years to come to the understanding that I presently have concerning OCD in my life. Like the peeling back of the layers of an onion, God has revealed things to me as I was ready for them and helped me in recognizing, accepting, and dealing with those revelations.

Because of the constant examination of my thoughts, words, and actions through the years, I had become too self-absorbed and introspective. An unhealthy perception of life developed out of my preoccupation of making sure that the bases were covered. I had not been consciously aware of the degree to which fear existed in my life.

My life wasn't spent doing it *all* wrong by any means. There was much love from a heart with good intentions. It's just that I have suffered needlessly along with my family and friends because of unhealthy thinking and behavior on my part. To the detriment of my children, I would scrutinize their behavior. I carried the responsibilities of parenthood too far and at times took on the role of conscience for my children instead of allowing them to live their own lives. They would get frustrated with me and justly so. Often, I interjected my two cents' worth when it wasn't warranted.

I have been robbed of joy, peace of mind, and happiness. My childhood thoughts were much too serious. Through the years, my own thoughts, words, and actions have at times been a hindrance to me being a shining light of the glory of the gospel of Jesus. On the inside, I was a mess.

Thankfully, I have progressed a long way from where I was, and with God's help, I will continue to make progress and experience more and more firsthand the abundant life that Jesus came to give us. What I have experienced in my life with God is very real. God did a transforming work in my life, and His Word is true. I want others to know and experience for themselves *what* and, more important, *Whom* I have come to know. You truly can be free from horrible bondage to OCD.

CHAPTER 2

God's Voice and Three Dreams

I woke up one morning and distinctly heard words. It might not have been a matter of hearing in the natural, the way that we hear with our fleshly ears, because there was no flesh-and-bones person there speaking to me. I'm not sure just how to describe it. Is it called hearing with your spirit? However you describe it, I distinctly *heard* words something like, "Truth shall set you free."

At first, I wondered what the words meant. Later, I was listening to a speaker on the Christian radio. He said something about truth. I thought maybe *that* was what I was meant to hear, and so I ordered a copy of the audio presentation.

But I also had a series of three dreams with a time interval in between each.

In the first dream, I was by myself, and I discovered that I had something in the end of my finger on my left hand. It has been a long time since I had the dreams, so I might not remember all of the details precisely. I tried to get it out, using the fingers on my right hand.

Time went by, and I had a second dream. This time, I had something in the fleshy part of my left hand just below the joints where the fingers connect to the hand. I was in the presence of a doctor. At first, he didn't see the problem, and then he did. I might have proceeded to try to get it out of my hand.

Time passed again, and I had the third dream. This time, I was by myself. I now had what appeared to be *bands* of worms in the underside of my arm below the elbow. The worms were black, very skinny, flat, and joined together side by side. In the dream, I was matter-of-factly pulling the bands of worms out of my arm.

These dreams were not simply goofy dreams. I have had regular dreams, and I have had goofy dreams that make me wonder, *Why did I dream that?* But I also have had what I call "God-given" dreams. I believe these three dreams were of that type.

Through the years, God has spoken to people through dreams. Joseph, son of Jacob, was given two dreams foretelling the role he would play in the deliverance of his family many years hence. Through a dream, an angel spoke to another Joseph after he found out that Mary was going to have a baby. The magi received a dream so that they wouldn't go back to Herod, and even Pilate's wife had a bad dream prior to the crucifixion of Jesus.

The prophet Joel said in Joel 2:28–29 that by the Spirit of the living God, God would move mightily in the lives of His people in supernatural ways. One of those ways would be through dreams.

I started counseling with a Christian counselor and related the dreams to him. I found out about OCD, went on medication, and was counseled on a regular basis for a period of time. At the time, I guessed that the worms signified all of the numerous things that I obsessed about or the resulting compulsive actions. At home, I made a *long* list of the things in my life that I thought might be connected with the OCD.

As time went on, I began to think that the worms represented something more. Yes, they represented all of the goofy thought and behavior patterns connected with OCD, but they represented more than that. They represented all of the mixed-up thinking and behavior in my life, some of which were catalysts to OCD-like behavior. The third dream indicated me eradicating these unhealthy menaces from my life.

CHAPTER 3

The Good News of Salvation

Bound by Fear

I was told that OCD is an anxiety disorder. I have had a lot of fear in my life. At the time that I learned about OCD, I did not realize just *how much* fear I had had in my life. I'm not sure that I even yet know, but I do have a greater realization of the extent than I used to have. One of my biggest fears was that of going to hell. My concern about going to hell was a legitimate one. However, God does not want us to live in unhealthy fear. Fear is not of God—*reverential* fear, yes, but *afraid* fear, no. I have heard it said that 365 times in the Bible, God tells us not to fear. That's enough times to cover each day of the year. Because I did not know God's answer to my fear, I adopted unhealthy ways to deal with it. These unhealthy patterns helped me to cope and maybe even helped to lift some of the burden, but they did not get to the root of my problem.

Truth Shall Set You Free[2]

Jesus says in John 8:31–32 that if we are His followers and continue to spend time in His word, He won't leave us in the dark, wondering what's going on or what we are to do. He will reveal truth to us, and that truth will be the missing piece to the puzzle; that truth will shoot down the lies of the devil. I desperately needed truth, truth to set me free. What is truth? Where do we find truth? Jesus is truth (John 14:6). God's word is truth (Psalm 119:160).

Jesus is the Word of God spoken in the Bible (John 1:1). Inevitably, it would be the Word of God that would liberate me. It was the Word of God that was able to cut through all the mess in my life and get to the heart of the issue. The words found in the Bible aren't equivalent to the words found in a newspaper, periodical, thesis, or textbook. They are alive and powerful! (Hebrews 4:12). Just like an antibiotic is beneficial to the human body, God's Word is meant to do us good in every area of our lives and every aspect of our being—our spirits, souls, and bodies.

The Bible is not just like any other book. Although it includes all of the following, it goes *beyond* history, stories, proverbs for daily living, and biographies, especially that of Jesus. The Bible truly contains God's words for mankind. Just as our physical bodies cannot live without proper food and water, we are dependent upon taking in God's words if we truly want to live our best lives, the lives that we dream about (Deuteronomy 8:3).

Ephesians 2:8–9

The passage from the Word of God that was so instrumental in my initial release from the horrible bondage that I was in is Ephesians 2:8–9. It makes me smile even as I read the words now:

> For by grace you have been saved through faith;
> and that not of yourselves, *it is* the gift of God;
> not as a result of works that no one should boast.

These Scriptures have been some of the most life-transforming for me! I repeated and memorized these verses. They impacted my life greatly. They helped set me free from the burden of trying to be good enough and do the right things, a burden that I had carried for years. No matter how hard I tried, I knew that I wasn't good enough. In fact, the harder I tried, the more messed-up I became.

The following is a dissection and elaboration of these verses.

> *"For by grace …"*

I've heard *grace* described as "unmerited favor." Salvation is not earned. We didn't do anything good enough to obtain it. It is a *gift* for us to accept and forever say thank you for with our lives by living for Jesus. When we realize that we could never make it to heaven on our own, that Jesus paid the price for our sins so that we could have eternal life not only in this lifetime here on earth but forever after with Him in heaven, and that he offers this gift freely unto us, we are sincerely grateful and *want* to live for Him.

> *"… you have been saved …"*

Our Need for a Savior

All of mankind who has ever walked the face of this earth, except for Jesus, has been in need of a savior. None of us has lived faultlessly (Romans 3:23). Because of our sins, we deserved the death penalty (Romans 6:23). Jesus is the only person who has never sinned, even though He experienced temptations just like we do (Hebrews 4:15).

Man was created with free will. God never has and never will violate our free will. He does not want our love for Him or devotion to Him to be feigned or forced. Satan came on the scene and tempted Eve. She and Adam both violated a direct order from God; the world has never been the same since.

Truly, God and heaven are real, and Satan and hell are real. We have a very real enemy, and a real spiritual battle takes place unseen by the natural eye. There are two sides in this spiritual war, God's and Satan's. The devil is out for our demise in every way, and Jesus is our victor over Satan. Satan schemes to come against all that is good, and God our Creator desires us to live truly good and fulfilling lives (Ephesians 6:11–12, John 10:10).

Jesus is clear when He tells us that it is only through Him that we are able to connect with our heavenly Father (John 14:6). Some may think, "That's narrow-mindedness." It is narrow-minded in the sense that Jesus *is* the only way. In man's way of thinking, it would be great if mankind could reach God through multiple avenues, but that is not reality. It is not truth. God the Father, God the Son, and God the Holy Spirit opened their heart wide when Jesus came and gave His life on our behalf.

Life on this earth is temporal. There is more, much more. When you leave this world, you go into eternity. The real you presently lives inside of your body. It's like your body is your house in which the real you dwells (2 Corinthians 5:6–8). It is not God's will or His desire for any person to end up in hell; it is His desire that we spend eternity with Him (2 Peter 3:9). Thanks be to God that all of mankind's need for a savior is met in the person of Jesus Christ.

Jesus, Our Savior

Salvation is found and promised in Jesus (Romans 10:13). The devil wreaked havoc upon the earth and brought much destruction to and in the lives of men. Jesus is the greatest supernatural

Superhero of all time! He came to stop the enemy in his tracks (1 John 3:8). Because of His great love for us, Jesus came to save us, not condemn us! (John 3:16–17).

The remedy for the sin factor of Adam and Eve and all mankind would be through the shed blood of a lamb on Calvary. Only through *blood* would the sins of mankind be forgiven (Hebrews 9:22). The numerous animal sacrifices of the Old Testament were a foreshadowing of the perfect sacrifice to come in the New Testament. This perfect sacrifice to come would not entail just any blood or just any lamb. It would be holy blood from the spotless Lamb, Jesus. Jesus is the only Lamb found worthy for such a sacrifice of blood (Revelation 5:12–13).

Salvation is a matter of God coming down in the person of His precious Son, Jesus, to save mankind from their sins. Salvation is about Jesus. It's all about Jesus (Colossians 1:18). No matter our background, ethnicity, or status, when we are saved, we become identified in Jesus (Colossians 3:11).

Our salvation is a matter of whether we *know* Jesus and are *known* by Him. It's a matter of relationship. Jesus is a real person. Maybe you attend a Christian denomination and are acquainted with the words of Jesus being our Savior, Redeemer, Son of God, Lord, and Good Shepherd. But do you *know* Him *personally* by these titles?

It's comparable to knowing *of* Dr. So-and-so or knowing him more personally by being a patient of his. You go to his office, speak with him face to face, and tell him what kind of physical problems you are having; he thus prescribes a course of treatment for you. You and the doctor have interaction with each other. Thus, you *know* him, not just know *of* him, and he knows you.

It's kind of the same thing with Jesus but, oh, with such greater depth! He desires for us to *know* Him, not just know *of* Him, and He wants to know us, in an intimate fashion. It is His heart's desire to be involved and welcome in every area of our lives. He is a person of the triune Godhead. God is the one who made us and desires to help us always (Isaiah 44:2). He is the potter; we are His masterpieces (Isaiah 64:8). He knows that man came from dust (Psalm 103:14, Genesis 2:7). Nothing in our lives is too big or too small for His attention. He is omniscient. He is well-acquainted with the activity of every single bird all over the world. At the same time, He knows every minute detail of our lives, with precision accuracy, interpretation, and understanding, including our molecular structure, DNA, and every thought, emotion, and experience that we have had or ever will have. He knows us better than we know ourselves (Matthew 10:29–31).

> "... *through faith; ...*"

Faith is belief. This kind of faith is not mere mental knowledge, as when reading facts in a book and believing those statements to be true. Saving faith, genuine faith, is a matter of the *heart* (Romans 10:10). It goes beyond simply believing that God exists; even the devil believes in God's existence, but that kind of faith does not save him (the devil) (James 2:19). Romans 10:8–11 explains that true faith involves the heart, and what is in our hearts will come out of our mouths.

> "... *and that not of yourselves, ... not as a result of works that no one should boast.*"

Salvation is not ...

A Matter of Law

It is not possible for you and me to keep all the laws, whatever they may be, even if we wanted to. I have heard of the analogy of a pie, but I will deviate and use a dish for an example. Think of a dish with imaginary sections. If there is a crack in any section of the dish, the dish is broken. It is broken in the *one* section, but it also makes the dish, as a *whole*, broken. James 2:10–11 explains that if we break any *one* of God's laws, we have become a violator.

Our salvation is *not* a matter of dos and don'ts, a list of laws or regulations to be followed, a checklist. One positive outcome of God's Law is that it helps us to *recognize* when we have done wrong (Romans 3:20). Through this recognition comes the additional realization that we need a Savior, thus bringing us to Jesus. The whole purpose of God's Law is to bring each one of us into relationship with Jesus (Galatians 3:24). A one-on-one, intimate relationship with Jesus is our ultimate goal (Romans 10:4). Jesus is the only one capable of keeping God's Law perfectly. The fulfillment of God's laws is accomplished in His Son (Matthew 5:17–18).

A Matter of Being/Doing Good

Someone might be thinking, *But I'm a good person.* By what or whose standards? A popular thought is *Well, it's not like I've killed anybody or anything like that.* Salvation is not *relative* to another's words or actions. It is not based on a sliding scale. Our salvation is *not* a matter of living a good, moral life *or* a matter of weighing our thoughts, words, and actions and counting on the good outweighing the bad.

We all need Jesus. He said that even people who do wrong also do loving and well-intentioned things for their family, friends, and others who reciprocate in kind to them, but God does not want us to remain under the classification of "sinners" (Luke 6:32–34). He came to rescue us from ourselves and our poor choices and from the devil's grasp and influence (Luke 19:10). When we RSVP "yes" to the invitation of God, we change camps, and our identity is simultaneously changed. We go from *sinner* to *saint* (1 Corinthians 1:1–2).

God is not throwing out good, purposeful, and kind things for us to do; they are just that—good and purposeful to the benefit of others, ourselves, and His kingdom. Ephesians 2:10 states that God made us and, in His infinite wisdom, preordained good things for each of us to do. However, our good, kind, and upright displays of love do not *save* us; they are as "filthy rags" when it comes to our salvation.

> But we are all as an unclean *thing*, and all our righteousnesses *are* as filthy rags; …
> —Isaiah 64:6 (KJV)

A Matter of Denominational Title

Salvation is *not* a matter of being named by any particular denominational title. Affiliation with a Christian denomination is good, but that alone will guarantee no man entrance into the kingdom of heaven. God does not want our denominational names to cause discord, disunity, and dividing walls. Just as *we* like it when all of our family members get along well with one another, our heavenly Father God likewise desires unity within *His* family, the global church (1 Corinthians 1:10–13).

A Matter of Us Saving Ourselves

Remember, we do not save ourselves. If that were the case, there would have been no need for God to willingly give His precious beloved Son to come and die a horrible death in our stead at Golgotha over two thousand years ago (John 3:16). If there were any other way that our salvation could have been attained, the death of God's Son could have been avoided.

Man, apart from the very Spirit of God Himself dwelling

within, doesn't do and live life the same way God does; nor is man's thought and reasoning process the same caliber as God's. His intellect is so superior to ours (Isaiah 55:8–9). The world's system says *you did the crime; you do the time.* God's system says *you did the crime*; Jesus *took your place and paid the price for your freedom.*

Our salvation cannot be *bought* by monetary contributions to any church or religious organization or even to the poor. There is no way possible to *earn* our salvation by doing enough good or by achieving higher levels of spirituality. No amount of suffering, sacrifice, offerings, or anything else on our part can *attain* our salvation.

Lost within the Church

If you're trying to approach God by formula alone and not with your *heart*, it is even possible to go to church and go through all the right motions, say all the right-sounding words, and be lost and not even know it. Jesus spoke of this type of situation regarding the religious elite of His day (Matthew 5:20). It is the condition of the *heart* that makes all the difference (Proverbs 4:23).

> You hypocrites, rightly did Isaiah prophesy of you, saying,
> "This people honors Me with their lips,
> But their heart is far away from Me.
> But in vain do they worship Me,
> Teaching as doctrines the precepts of men."
> (Matthew 15:7–9)

Just as in the professional arena, there are the real and the fake, in Christendom, there are also the true and false Christians. Jesus addressed this truth in the parable in Matthew 13:24–30 when He spoke of bad weeds that grew up with the wheat. These bad weeds started off looking similar to the real deal.

The litmus test of whether one is a true Christian is one of *relationship* with the Most High God. How sad it would be for one to live one's whole life *thinking* that one is on track, just to find out that one wasn't. Jesus spoke of such people in Matthew 7:22–23. They spoke religious-ese and did outwardly religious acts in Jesus's name but in the future would be disappointed and surprisedly so.

In 2 Corinthians 13:5, we are encouraged to consider our position with God and to be bold enough to check it out to see whether it is genuine.

"... it is the gift of God; ..."

Our heavenly Father gave us the "gift" of His most precious Son, Jesus. Jesus willingly obeyed His Father, left His Father and His heavenly abode, and came to earth in the form of a little fleshly baby to live and walk the face of this earth among sinful mankind and to die for us in our stead so that we could know and live firsthand the abundant life that He came to give us. How great a love God has for us! (John 15:13). Jesus, who is God incarnate, temporarily set aside His supernatural godly abilities and powers to live a brief fleshly existence here on earth just like you and me. He walked in humility and obedience to His Father, which included dying on our behalf (Philippians 2:5–8).

Salvation for You

Personal Salvation Experience

Some people can tell you the exact time and place of their salvation experience. I cannot—not pinpoint-specifically. I *can* remember as a little girl playing church in the entryway of our two-story home. I also recall, as a young girl, being on my bed, looking up toward the night sky and talking to God.

As I was growing up, I tried to pay attention to the words I voiced as I said my prayers; I didn't want to merely *say* prayers and not give heed to what I was saying. I'm guessing I was in my upper teens when I went to confession and confessed my lack of prayer; in justification, I voiced my failure to even *think* about it sometimes. I had failed to recognize (and the priest brought it to my attention) that *that* was part of the problem. My failure to even *think* about praying indicated that something was wrong. There was a deeper issue than my lack of prayer; it was the lack of desire in my heart to pray. When you have a good relationship with someone, you enjoy spending time and doing things with him or her and talking with each other.

I tried to do right, but there were times when I definitely sinned. I went to church regularly, but I did not truly know the gospel message of salvation. Once I started to understand God's plan of salvation for me, it was like a breath of fresh air! It was a pivotal point in my life. Even then, I didn't fully comprehend God's plan of salvation, but God's Holy Spirit had given me enough revelation to make a huge difference in my life.

Prayer of Salvation

There is no specific formula to follow to ask Jesus to be your Savior. Years ago, I participated in an adult Sunday school class. There came a time when a pretty young lady with blond hair, who had been attending the same class as I, expressed to me her desire to know Jesus as her Savior. I was afraid of handling it incorrectly (fear again) and referred her to the pastor, who was the teacher of the class.

When asking Jesus to be your Savior, the main thing is the attitude and sincerity of your heart and that *you* ask Him.

> [F]or with the heart man believes, resulting in righteousness, and with the mouth he confesses, resulting in salvation.
> —Romans 10:10

Luke 23:39–43 relates the story of Jesus dying upon the cross with two criminals, one on either side of him. One of the criminals ultimately embraced Jesus. His words weren't complicated, and Jesus honored them. Jesus will not force Himself upon anyone. He wants us to come to Him freely and freely of our own accord to invite Him into our lives (Revelation 3:20).

A suggested prayer might be, "Jesus, I'm a sinner. I have sinned many, many times in my life. I'm asking You to be my Lord and Savior and forgive me of my sins and save me from sin, hell, and the devil. I ask You, Jesus, to come and live in my heart and clean up my life and help me to live for You forever. I will eternally be thankful. Amen."

To ask Jesus to be your "Lord" is to ask Him to be the Master and Ruler of your life. You relinquish the controls of your life to Him and surrender everything in your life to Him, His way, and His will. As you progress in your walk with the Lord, His Holy Spirit will help you in this process.

A Fresh Start / New Life in Him

If you prayed this prayer, God has blessed you with a new life in Him (Revelation 21:5). He has blessed you with a fresh start, a new beginning (Psalm 103:12). In fact, He continually blesses us with fresh starts, new beginnings, each and every day! He is the God of "do-overs."

You may still have to experience some of the *consequences* of poor choices from your past for a while, but He will even bring *good* out of all of the bad stuff in your life, whether it was bad that *you* did or bad done *to you* by someone else. Who but God could do that? (Romans 8:28). God is God of the impossible—what *seems* impossible to our natural senses, reasoning minds, and life as we have known it (Luke 18:27).

God will bring order where there has been chaos, peace where there has been turmoil, truth where there has been confusion, and joy no matter what the circumstances; for that is what His kingdom looks like (Romans 14:17). He desires all these good things for us, because He knows that true happiness, true living, starts on the inside (Luke 17:21).

Psalm 103 sums up this chapter beautifully!

> Bless the Lord, O my soul;
> And all that is within me, *bless* His holy name.
> Bless the Lord, O my soul,
> And forget none of His benefits;
> Who pardons all your iniquities;
> Who heals all your diseases;
> Who redeems your life from the pit;
> Who crowns you with lovingkindness and compassion;
> Who satisfies your years with good things,
> *So that* your youth is renewed like the eagle.
> The Lord performs righteous deeds,
> And judgments for all who are oppressed.
> He made known His ways to Moses,
> His acts to the sons of Israel.
> The Lord is compassionate and gracious,
> Slow to anger and abounding in lovingkindness.
> He will not always strive *with us*;
> Nor will He keep *His anger* forever.
> He has not dealt with us according to our sins,
> Nor rewarded us according to our iniquities.
> For as high as the heavens are above the earth,

So great is His lovingkindness toward those who fear Him.
As far as the east is from the west,
So far has He removed our transgressions from us.
Just as a father has compassion on *his* children,
So the LORD has compassion on those who fear Him.
(Psalm 103:1–13)

CHAPTER 4

Born Again

Scripture Reference

Once you have received Jesus into your heart, you have been "born again." Many are familiar with these words or have at least heard this expression, which is taken from the Gospel of John 3:3:

> Jesus answered and said to him, "Truly, truly, I say to you, unless one is born again, he cannot see the kingdom of God."

This born-again experience happens by the Spirit, the Holy Spirit, of the Most High God. It truly is a supernatural experience initiated by God Himself; it is not something man does solely of his own accord or comes up with on his own (John 3:6–8).

Brand-New You

Now there is a brand-new you.

> Therefore if any man is in Christ, *he* is a new creature; the old things passed away; behold, new things have come. (2 Corinthians 5:17)

The word *new* here comes from the Greek word (2537) "*kainos*," which means "qualitatively new as contr. with *neos* (3501), numerically new or the last one numerically."[3] It isn't simply a matter that God has *changed* you; you truly are a new and different you. God changes us from the inside out.

As time progresses, you will recognize for yourself that you aren't the same person you used to be. I was probably eighteen years old when, around Halloween time, I dressed up in a witch's costume just for the fun of it. Now I have no desire to do that. I presently have a better knowledge and understanding of the satanic realm and the evil forces that are at work in this world. I mention this story to say, "That was then, and this is now." This is just one example of the many ways in which God has truly changed me and *continues* to change me. I am no longer the same as I was then.

When one is born again, the Spirit of the Most High God takes up residence within that person's very being, and *He* begins to change him or her. God Himself will let each individual know that which He wants him or her to do or not do, how to live his or her life (Romans 8:14). God's Spirit will lead and guide us in our walk with Him while we are in this world and even beyond this life as we know it.

Change will be instantaneous with the moment of salvation, but all the changes that need to be made and that God desires to make in us *may not*, and most likely *will not*, take place all at once. If the faith is genuine, change *will* take place; it is inevitable. Your language will change. Your tastes in entertainment will change. How you choose to spend your time will change. You will no longer use the excuse that *everybody else does it*. Your very demeanor will change. People will inevitably see a new you.

Prayer will not be merely a chore or a task on your to-do list but an honor and a privilege. The Word of God will be music to your ears. Your love for people will grow. You will pray for your enemies instead of cursing them. You will choose to suffer instead of taking revenge by your own hand. You will develop compassion for and be hopeful for the lost instead of considering someone as a good-for-nothing. You will see through the eyes of Christ instead of merely through the eyes of flesh. Those who are His will love His words.

From a Child of Flesh to a Child of God

We are all God's *creation*, but not all are God's *children* (Romans 9:8). Upon being born again, we are adopted as God's children (Galatians 4:4–6).

From Death to Life

Prior to being born again, we were dead spiritually and lived liked everybody else. We catered to what *we* wanted—if it seemed good, felt good, sounded good, made sense to *us*, exhilarated the senses, was in vogue, didn't seem to be hurting anybody else, we did it, unaware we were following the devil. That doesn't mean that everything we thought, said, and did was evil; however, when we *were* off course, we were advancing Satan's agenda (Ephesians 2:1–3).

Although we did not know that we were spiritually dead, we can be thankful a merciful God knew. He loves us so much that He *did* not and *does* not want to leave us there. He provided a way for us to come alive. His desire is to knock down and remove all of the barriers between Him and us and everything that stands in the way of us living great lives (Ephesians 2:4–7).

From Darkness to Light

Prior to the new birth, we were in darkness; now we are in the light (1 Peter 2:9). Not only were we *in* darkness, but we *were* darkness! (Ephesians 5:8). Our new lives are to line up with the change that has taken place within us.

From Satan's Dominion to the Kingdom of God

Not only were we *in* darkness and *were* darkness, but we were also under the influence of an evil dominion of which Satan is the head (Acts 26:18). We experience a mighty deliverance. We are now part of the kingdom of all kingdoms. Our allegiance is to all that God represents and away from an evil domain (Colossians 1:13–14).

Love originates with God (1 John 4:8). He is awesome! He is our Redeemer and our Savior, our Creator and the Creator of the heavens and the earth, the very universe! He is the one and only true and living God! He is God of new beginnings, fresh starts, and umpteenth chances! He *is* the beginning! He rescues us from the realm of Satan and his evil schemes and calls us unto Himself. He promises abundant life to those of us who know Him through His Son, Jesus. All that is good, our very lives, starts and ends in Him. The most important things in life are free—free to *us*; *He* paid the price (Revelation 21:6).

Abode and Role of the Holy Spirit

The Spirit of the very real and living God now lives on the inside of the person who has been born again. The Holy Spirit of the Most High God is our Helper. It is not our Father's will that we be on our own to do this thing called life. He, Himself, the very One who designed us and desired us to be, desires to be with us every second of our existence. It is not good enough for Him that He be *with* us; He has ordained it that He be *in* us by the power of His Spirit! His Spirit speaks nothing but truth. He is our perfect guide (John 14:16–18).

The Spirit of God is our teacher, and He is the best there is. He will teach us everything we need to know—everything from how to parent to how to be happily married, how to manage finances, and how to bake a cake. Even when we are taking a test (the tests of life), He gives us the answers that He has been teaching us; it's an open-book test! (John 14:26).

The Bible Comes Alive

This is why the Bible comes alive to the person who has been born again. The *Spirit* of the Word of God is the very One who is teaching what that Word is saying. What used to seem to be nonsense to the unregenerate person (one who has not been born again) now makes sense. What he formerly viewed as words upon a printed page, a compilation of history, genealogy, and biography, reserved primarily for the formal church setting of Sunday morning pews and pulpits, now has become alive and makes sense to the born-again reader. Apart from the illumination of the Holy Spirit, a person *can't* make sense of the Holy Scriptures even if he or she wants to. It's like the Holy Spirit is the Code Decipher-er. Now that the born-again Christian has the Holy Spirit, he or she has the necessary Person to unlock the vast hidden wealth contained in the Bible (1 Corinthians 1:18, 2:14).

This understanding does not come all at once but continues to unfold. It is a progressive transformation (2 Corinthians 3:18). The Spirit explains the symbolism in the Bible and connects the writings of the Old Testament with the New Testament. It is like a multifaceted gem; the more we look, the more we see. One could never exhaust the treasure of wealth found in the Bible in this lifetime. With the guidance of the Holy Spirit, the born-again believer can hear, in his or her spirit, God speaking to him or her through the Word of God. Now, reading the Bible is not drudgery and instead becomes something that you look forward to with anticipation. The very words of God never grow old. There is always a fresh word and new insight to be revealed in the Word.

Not of This World

The born-again Christian who continues to grow in the Lord no longer fits the mold of this present world and its system. He or she stands out among the crowd (1 Peter 2:9). Just as we may not always understand the movements and dynamics of the wind, others may not understand why the born-again person does, thinks, and lives the way he or she does (John 3:8). They may think he or she is the odd duck out and say some not-so-good things about him or her (1 Peter 4:4). He or she may even be hated (John 17:14–16). This world is not our final destination; it is a temporary address (1 Peter 2:11).

Earth is the locale for our temporary assignment from God to be His ambassadors (2 Corinthians 5:20). We are here on purpose—for God's purposes, reaching out to the world, our sphere of influence. We are God's representatives in this earth, speaking for Him and living for Him, being His feet to go, knees to be in a position of prayer, hands to help, arms to hug and bear the burdens of others, eyes to see with compassion, ears to patiently listen, and hearts to love unselfishly and forgive.

Heaven Is Home

Heaven is now our real home, and until it is time for us to go home, we remain here to do the will of the Father who is in heaven. The born-again person is seated in heaven (Ephesians 2:4–6).

Chapter 11 in the book of Hebrews tells of men and women of great faith who preceded us in sojourning in this world as foreigners. It also speaks of a land for which they longed, one not of the earthly realm (Hebrews 11:13–16). Jesus has gone on ahead of us.

When we join Him in heaven, all the preparations on our behalf will have been made. He desires that ultimately we be with Him (John 14:2–3).

You Are the "Righteousness of God"[4]

Having been raised Catholic, I was accustomed to going to confession. Even when I didn't go to confession, I was in the habit of confessing my sins to God and asking Him for forgiveness. After accepting Jesus as my personal Savior, I also continued to confess my sins to God and ask Him for forgiveness. Then just in the last number of years, I learned that all of my sins are forgiven, even ones that I haven't committed yet. What? How liberating! This has been revolutionary for me! Through the years, I had been *so* conscious of my sins!

Sometimes when I catch myself sinning, I will pray similarly, "Thank You, Lord, that my sins are forgiven. I'm sorry for ... Help me not to do that again. In Jesus's name, I pray. Amen." Take the focus off of yourself, and focus on God, who He is, and what He has done and continues to do for you. He loves you!

Any right standing that we have is *only* by the righteousness that is imputed to us by God because of our lives being hidden in Christ. When putting on my spiritual armor, sometimes I have said, "Thank you, Jesus, for bearing my sins upon the tree and in their stead, imparting your righteousness unto me."

> He made Him who knew no sin *to be* sin on our behalf,
> that we might become the righteousness of God in Him.
> —2 Corinthians 5:21

For not knowing about God's righteousness, and seeking to establish their own, they did not subject themselves to the righteousness of God. For Christ is the end of the law for righteousness to everyone who believes.
—Romans 10:3–4

Religion

Your born-again life is not merely a matter of "religion." Those who do not understand this whole *God thing* might look upon the person who has moved from the ways of the world to the kingdom of God as someone who "got religion."

It's like they are looking at this whole *God thing* from the outside in, kind of like a child at Christmastime, looking intently through the window of a toy store at all the toys inside. Looking in from the outside is not the same as experiencing from the inside. One might view a Christian as one who *does* and *does not* do certain things—a matter of following certain rituals, customs, dos and don'ts, and laws, whether God's or man's. But it's oh *so* much more! It's relationship with God Himself!

The Abundant Life

As long as we are sinners and function in our *own* way of thinking instead of submitting ourselves under the Lordship of Jesus Christ, we will not live fully the great and wonderful lives we so desire. It's only in Christ that we find true fulfillment.

Jesus said to him, "I am the way, and the truth, and the life; ..."
—John 14:6

The word *life* here comes from the word *Zoe* in the Greek: "... expressing all of the highest and best which Christ is (Jn. 14:6; 1 Jn. 1:2) and which He gives to the saints. The highest blessedness of the creature."[5]

Our enemy, the devil, wants nothing but bad for us. He wants us and everybody and everything in our lives to be empty, dead, and ruined. Jesus wants just the opposite; He desires the very best for us and our loved ones. He wants us to have *great* lives (John 10:10).

In Christ, God makes it possible for each and every one of us to know firsthand experientially the good life that we're each searching for. The born-again Christian enters into that abundant life. It is a life of purpose and meaning, one of fulfillment, centered on Christ and His plan. Jesus, His Father, and His Holy Spirit make up the triune Godhead who is the Master Designer and Creator of it all. Jesus has been on the scene since the very beginning. He was involved in the creation process of all that is (John 1:1–4).

If you want to see God, look to Jesus. He is the very reason for our existence. No matter the topic, He is number One—period! No debate. He is our glue. (Colossians 1:15–18). Just as we look for the instructions when we purchase a product and undertake to assemble it, we look to the One who fashioned, designed, and made the unique persons we are for the instructions for *our* lives (Isaiah 51:1).

God gives the promise of bright tomorrows. All we have to do is accept this promise and choose to follow Him. Jeremiah 29:11 is one of my favorite verses in all of the Bible: "'For I know the plans that I have for you,' declares the LORD, 'plans for welfare and not for calamity to give you a future and a hope'" (Jeremiah 29:11).

He gives each and every one of us individual purpose and brings meaning to our lives. We are meant to be a blessing unto one another and bring glory to God. We are to be men, women, and children of excellent moral character (Ephesians 2:10; 1 Peter 2:12).

To follow Jesus is to know a life of righteousness, joy, and peace: "... for the kingdom of God is not eating and drinking, but righteousness and peace and joy in the Holy Spirit" (Romans 14:17). It is a *righteousness* that none on his or her own can achieve, a *peace* that is not of this world, a peace that only Jesus can give, and a *joy* that surmounts any tragedy or circumstance and endures the test of time (Isaiah 9:6).

CHAPTER 5

Truth

Truth Is Imperative

Whether you are facing OCD or some other obstacle, start with truth; it is imperative. If we believe a lie and are consequently living in response to that lie, we will not receive the results that we want. For example, if someone tells you that the bridge is out up ahead, but you don't believe it and proceed ahead anyway, you will eventually discover that the bridge *is*, in fact, out and be faced with a detour.

This is how it is for someone who deals with obsessive-compulsive disorder. Somehow or other, that person's thinking has become skewed; he or she is believing a lie, living in response to that lie, and not getting the results that he or she wants. This person is doing the best that he or she knows to do, and it's a struggle. His or her words and actions are in response to his or her way of thinking, and he or she does not realize at the onset that this thinking is off balance or unhealthy. As time progresses, an unhealthy pattern sets in, resulting in repeated unwanted results, and he or she comes to realize that something *is* wrong but may not be able to pinpoint just what the error is. He or she may even be able to identify the pattern of behavior that is indicative of the problem but still not be able to identify the source or cause of the problem in order to fix it—kind of like a car that continues to stall, but the mechanic just has not been able to pinpoint the cause or like a person who is plagued with chronic pain, but the doctors have not been able to come up with a reason why.

We can't live life by faulty patterns and expect to receive good results. If we live by healthy, balanced thinking and behavior, we will live healthy, balanced lives. If our basic premises and corresponding behaviors are skewed, our lives will be dysfunctional (Galatians 6:7–8).

Jesus Is Truth

In your quest for truth, start with Jesus, who *is* truth (John 14:6). If you have not yet done so, ask Jesus to be your Lord and Savior. Whether we realize it or not, this world functions according to God's laws, ways, and system; our denial or failure to recognize this truth does not alter the validity of this statement. To live optimally, we need to get ourselves in line with Him.

Many are following less beneficial pathways for their lives and are not experiencing the abundant life as God intended. They may be pursuing a career or an active social life, keeping up on the latest trends, following the entertainment circuit, or keeping sway with current talk shows. Many pursue a life of self-indulgence, reaping the gratification of today but not recognizing the fate of tomorrow. Seeking approval or following the advice of their counselor, friends, family, or latest TV guru are the inappropriate priorities of some.

Some of these things are not bad in and of themselves; some are even beneficial and biblically based when done God's way. It is when we put them above God and leave Him out of the picture or place Him farther on down the list that things don't work out. At the end of the day, we will feel empty if Jesus isn't in it.

Choices lacking in merit will leave us deficient. There are those who are making poor choices and reaping the consequences of those choices, not knowing that a better life truly is possible for them (Luke 18:27).

Consciously or not, some keep themselves very busy so that they won't have time to face the weightier matters of life that continue to be pushed down into the inner recesses of the soul; while others self-medicate or pursue other avenues to hide from the burdens and stress of this life.

How many are simply living mundane lives, making it through day by day with loss of aspirations and goals, unconsciously believing that dreams for today and the future have passed them by and have been relegated to remain packed away in the closet of their youth never to come their way again?

Many are following a false way of religion or belief system that gives an illusion of help but leaves them wanting for more. Some are a god unto themselves, and even *they* fail themselves.

Wisdom starts with God (Proverbs 1:7). God does not want us to be afraid of Him in a bad sense; after all, He is the very One who created us and desired us to exist, and He desires for each and every one of us to know Him intimately and He us, but He does desire for us to have a *reverential* fear of Him for who He is.

Believing in His existence is imperative, but we also need to believe in His character. We get to know His character through His Word, prayer, other believers, and our relationship and personal experiences with Him (Hebrews 11:6; Revelation 22:13).

We need to know which of many voices to heed and which to ignore (1 Corinthians 14:10). There are the voices of the occult, witchcraft, and Satan; the voices of approval and rejection; a voice of shame and one of elevation; a voice of self-hatred and despair and a voice of encouragement and hope; voices of truth and falsehood; a voice of defeat and a voice of triumph in the face of defeat—just to name a few. There are the voices of man and this world's system, and then there is the voice of God (Isaiah 49:1).

In your quest for truth, listen to and heed the voice of God, who is the very essence of truth.

> Jesus therefore was saying to those Jews who had believed Him, "If you abide in My word, *then* you are truly disciples of Mine; and you shall know the truth, and the truth shall make you free." (John 8:31–32)

Look to God for truth in every area of your life where you need freedom—from insurmountable guilt; unbearable shame; reproach from those closest to you or rejection from a spouse; the betrayal of a friend; condemnation whether from self, others, or the devil; hidden bondage; unspeakable despair; lingering sickness; hatred; unforgiveness from without and from within; self-destructive behavior; a sorrowful past; unimaginable abuse or neglect; an unhealthy lifestyle or choices; negative thinking; sadness and grief beyond measure; disparaging remarks; or ravaging damage caused by grave violations even from within the church to your spirit, soul, or body.

It is God's desire to bring freedom from whatever would hinder you in your walk with Him or prevent you from coming to know Him personally. This is our destiny in Christ Jesus (Galatians 5:13). Jesus is our Superhero who has come on the scene to conquer His archenemy and completely blow to smithereens all of the havoc he has wrought on the earth (1 John 3:8).

Isaiah 61 expresses beautifully the desire of God's heart toward those who would choose Him. Although not a complete compilation, the following are paraphrased from Isaiah 61: The anointing of God is upon Jesus to do awesomely beautiful things in our lives. When we're feeling down and out, He brings an encouraging word. Only through His love do we experience true healing for a broken heart.

He brings freedom when we are bound in any way. He blesses us with His beautiful favor. When we are wronged, He's got our back. When our souls are in the depths of sorrow and our dreams are a heap of ash, He comforts like no one else and brings beauty and happiness back into our lives. He keeps us from giving up when we are weak and raises us up like strong oak trees. All of this is because of His great love for us and so that our lives would bring glory to Him for who He is and rightly so. We will bring back that which was ruined. That which we thought to be devastated will be restored, even if it's been a long time coming. People we don't even know will do good things on our behalf because we are His. Without formal seminary education and training, we will be looked upon and deemed God's ministers. Resources from abroad will come to us. He will bless us with a double blessing for whatever wrong we have experienced. He gives us joy where we were humiliated and shamed. God is just. He is a covenant God. Because of the blessing of God, our descendants will not be obscure but well-known. We will be very happy people because of what our God has done on our behalf, and we will give credit to Him. Everything in our lives will be redeemed by His great love. When He sees us, He will see Jesus instead of our shortcomings. Just as a bridal couple, He is attractive to us, and we are lovely to Him. No nation will be without the touch of His great love.

How could one do anything but accept a benefit package such as that?

In your quest for truth, the first thing that you need to do is to go after God (Matthew 6:33). *Know* Jesus, not merely through your intellect but intimately in and with all of your heart (John 14:6). As you continue to read the words of God to you in the Bible and embrace the truth of those words, by His Spirit, He will do His part to reveal truth that you need to be freed from whatever would keep you bound (John 8:31–32). Having more sources of wise counsel available to you ensures a greater possibility of victory (Proverbs 11:14). However, God's Word is clear that we must keep

Him number one in our lives. Go to Him for truth above anybody else (Psalm 118:8–9).

God's Word Is Truth

Do you sometimes find yourself in the situation where you don't know what or whom to believe? It's possible to receive a diversity of opinions on any given subject from within your own family, circle of friends, scientific community, college professors, theologians, and local church congregation. You may be in the valley of decision at this moment, alternating between two or more differing viewpoints that are volleying back and forth within your own self. What do we use as a measuring tool to determine who's right and who's wrong, what to believe and what not to believe, which course is on track and which is not?

The words of the Bible are true; they are the very words of God Himself. The Bible is a sure word, a word that you can believe and put your trust in (Psalm 119:160; John 17:17). God's Word is what we need to separate truth from error, for it is a powerful weapon of delicate precision and accuracy, able to distinguish the falsehood that is sometimes so craftily disguised that it has the deception of being something good.

> For the word of God is living and active and sharper than any two-edged sword, and piercing as far as the division of soul and spirit, of both joints and marrow, and able to judge the thoughts and intentions of the heart. (Hebrews 4:12)

Truths contained within the pages of the Bible will shed light in the darkest areas of your life, and you don't have to be a theologian or highly educated to understand these truths (Psalm 119:130). God's word will illumine the right path (Psalm 119:105).

Scientific, anthropological, and geographical theories abound, but these as well as other speculations in medicine and philosophy are altered or negated from time to time as new revelations are uncovered. The words God speaks to us in the Bible are a constant upon which we can build and entrust our lives. His words will never go away or fade into the distant past (Isaiah 40:8). They have the backing of heaven itself, the highest seat of all judicial matters (Psalm 119:89). His words are strong, durable, and resilient; nothing can penetrate or destroy them. They have continued to live on in the face of the greatest trials and have stood and will continue to stand the test of time (Psalm 18:30; Proverbs 30:5). He has made His word great! (Psalm 138:2).

The Spirit of Truth[6]

When Jesus lived in bodily form upon the earth, masses of people sought Him out, followed Him, and longed to be with Him. He knew that it was the will of His heavenly Father that He would be returning to His Father from whence He had come (John 8:14 KJV). Although Jesus was going to return to heaven to be with His Father, man on earth was not going to be left to fend for himself against the wiles of the devil. Jesus's physical departure from earth might have seemed to be a loss for His disciples and loved ones, but it was actually to their advantage. While Jesus walked this earth, He was not able to be physically present everywhere at one time. Through His departure and His Spirit's coming, the very Spirit of God Himself would be able to be not just *with* but *within* every Christian everywhere at all times (John 16:7).

> And I will ask the Father, and He will give you another Helper, that He may be with you forever; *that* is the Spirit of truth, whom the world cannot receive, because it does not behold Him or know

> Him, *but* you know Him because He abides with you, and will be in you. I will not leave you as orphans; I will come to you. (John 14:16–18)

The Spirit of the Most High God Himself is the very agent who imparts truth to us wherever and whenever it is needed. He is our guide in the present day, into the unknown future, and through the murky waters of confusion and deception (John 16:13). What better source for instruction than the One who fashioned us and designed the world in which we live, the very Creator of the universe!

The Holy Spirit is not limited as to how He is able to communicate to us that which we need to know. He is not limited to functions of time and space and natural earthly laws, all elements of His own design. He may speak to us through dreams and visions, our hearts and intellect, the spoken or printed Word, other people, and nature itself. The possibilities are endless. He spoke to Balaam through a donkey (Numbers 22:1–24:25) and got Jonah's attention through a fish (Jonah 1:1–2:10)!

CHAPTER 6

Fear

I have been told that OCD is an anxiety disorder. If you are wrestling with OCD, I encourage you to think of what may be the source of that anxiety in your life. You might even find that it is a combination of things. Once you have pinpointed the source, look for truth regarding that source.

A good part of the anxiety in my life was fear-based. I have had a lot of fear. Not until my adult life did I realize just how *much* fear I have had. I don't know if I even yet realize the full extent of the fear that I have had. Starting when I was young, I developed a big fear of going to hell. What an overwhelming fear for a young girl to deal with! That particular fear definitely comprised part of the foundation of anxiety underlying OCD in my life; the groundwork was being laid for a messed-up life. This is a perfect example of why truth is imperative. Had I known that my salvation could not be achieved by being good enough but instead could be mine for the asking, I would have been spared a ton of heartache and grief (Ephesians 2:8).

The underlying premise for any thought or action is very pertinent. If the underlying premise is flawed, the outcome of the response based upon such a premise will also be flawed—the greater the flaw, the more the outcome will also be flawed.

You don't expect to pick strawberries from poison ivy. If you want to pick strawberries, you go to a strawberry patch; the fruit matches the plant. Good things come from safe and healthy plants; bad things come from weeds and dangerous plants (Matthew 7:16–18). In the same way, just as produce is directly correlated to the kind of seed that was put into the ground, the unfolding of our present-day lives is in large part a direct result of the life choices that we have made, both big and small (Galatians 6:7).

Also, the greater the *gravity* of the subject matter, the greater the potential for flawed solutions, because the desire to find a solution will be in direct proportion to the gravity of the subject matter at hand. Desperation can be an ominous factor when problem solving.

In my case, it was a matter of a *very* serious nature—the knowledge of the *reality* of hell, a limited but albeit sufficient knowledge of the *nature* of hell, and the awareness of the possibility of me ending up there after my time upon earth. Because of the depth of the seriousness of such an issue, I responded with a correlating depth of attention to what I perceived to be the solution. However, my solution for such a dilemma was very flawed, and thus I reaped a very flawed conclusion—me being very messed up with OCD, among other things, which are elaborated upon within this book. Whether the OCD *preceded* the fear of hell that I had (*Which came first, the chicken or the egg?*), I do not know. This I know, the fear that I had and the OCD were definitely connected.

If you are dealing with OCD, chances are that you can think of a correlating event (or events) that occurred at the onset of OCD in your life, and you might also be aware of underlying factors that you think are associated somehow with the presence of OCD. Consider if there is an underlying traumatic event that occurred in your life that you believe has a bearing upon how you view and deal with life today. Maybe there was no one particular trauma that took place, but instead, it was the environment in which you were raised. Maybe it was abuse or neglect or half-truths and half-lies that were indoctrinated into your mind. Whatever the unpleasant memory may be, give careful consideration as to how those circumstances impacted your life then and have continued to reverberate through the years to the present.

Next, talk to God about everything, and ask Him to be your Counselor (Isaiah 9:6). He desires to be your *personal* Counselor, and He will be the best one that you will ever have. He knows you better than you know yourself and is intimately acquainted with every detail of your life. Not only is He intimately acquainted with every detail of your life, but He is also intimately acquainted with every minute detail of the circumstances of your past, present, and in between and also with every person involved in the whole mess. He knows exactly what took place and where and when and why and how. His recall is perfect, whereas we sometimes remember through rose-colored glasses and self-righteousness, hateful revenge, and childhood thinking patterns that never moved on to maturity. Sometimes, we harbor shame, guilt, resentment, and hurt so deep that our conscious mind does not want to acknowledge it. Ask Him to reveal the truth that you need in order to be set free from whatever it is that has you bound—that is, whatever continues to feed the fear.

In connection with the faulty thinking and behavioral patterns that you know you have, pay attention to the underlying thoughts that motivate them. Don't just stop at *I don't know why I do what I do*. Go deeper, pursue the *why*, and listen. After receiving the answer to *one* question, you might have to ask why a number of times in order to uncover all of the layers until you get to the source.

Once you know the *why*, consider that answer as your starting point and begin the messed-up part of your life over. Recognize the thought process that developed way back then. Also recognize relevant factors that impacted your course of thinking that developed at that time—age of maturity, intense physical or emotional pain, unbearable grief, total shock, horrendous assault of the body or soul, intense loneliness, insurmountable guilt, vulnerability at the hands of someone in a position of authority, abuse by someone or an institution that is commonly thought of as trustworthy, domineering or controlling authority figures, the absence of love or a deep wound of rejection by someone you love, and so on. The list of possible factors is endless.

If you were young, realize that the avenue that your mind chose at that time to deal with the situation may not have been the best one, even though it may have been the best that you knew. If the same set of circumstances were to reoccur in your life now, chances are you would choose to handle the situation differently. The traumatic event, injustice, and so on would still be painful, but you would choose to react or respond differently, because you are not the same person that you were then. Now you have the maturity to recognize that there are alternative choices that you were unaware of way back then. Over the years, you got stuck in a rut, stuck in the mind-set that you chose at such an early age. It's like you chose a course of action, dug in with both heels, and got stuck, and you're still there twenty years later.

Ask yourself what form of fear presented itself at that time in the past and continues to fuel the turmoil in your present. Be bold to face that fear head-on and accept and receive the truth regarding your circumstances so that you can experience a new freedom (John 8:32). I've heard it said that the Bible states 365 times for us not to be afraid. That's one time for every day of the year. It is also indicative of the intensity with which fear can be our enemy. Oppressive, intimidating, paralyzing, life-draining fear is not of God. We are meant to walk in a God-based power and be loving toward God, ourselves, and others. An abundant life includes peace of mind as we live our days (2 Timothy 1:7 KJV).

To any and all who would accept Him, you have been handpicked by God Himself. Because of His presence with us, we don't need to be anxious or live in fear. He is on His throne and above the troubles of this world. When our strength is waning, we find new strength in Him. He takes us by the hand and helps us. He comes to our aid whenever we are faced with anger and contentions from others. He rescues us from quarrelsome and warring factions; it is His desire that our lives be peaceful. When we feel like we're about as low as we can go, He assures us over and over again we do not need to be afraid and that He is there to help us. He is our Redeemer for every circumstance (Isaiah 41:8–14).

Facing that fear may be unpleasant at first, but God will strengthen you. When you begin to know God, His character, who He is, and the depth of His love for you, you will rest comfortably and peacefully in His loving arms, and the fear will fall away. It is like the refining of gold. If there is an element of fear, one does not yet have an accurate interpretation of God's love (1 John 4:18).

This pure love comes from God Himself. Only *He* can love us with such pure and peaceful love that we are no longer afraid. Do not look to others for this kind of love. No person on earth, no matter how close to God, will love us faultlessly. Even though people may be born again and have the Spirit of the living God residing inside of them, they are still human. We all fail. In the course of the ups and downs of daily living, look to the lover and maker of your soul for the kind of love that will never disappoint or let you down.

If you are afraid of going to hell, afraid of rejection, afraid of "doing it wrong," afraid of making a mistake, or live under a pervading cloud of fear all day long, choose God's love for you and the truth He reveals to you, whether personally or through His Word, and allow that love and truth to take precedence over those fears. Allow God's voice to have authority over the voices of death, doom, and gloom in your life. When the devil brings to your remembrance some hurtful remark that someone has said to you, replace that thought with truth from God's Word.

I'm certain that fear is one of the devil's most lethal weapons against us, but we who are in Christ have victory over fear. We are not doomed to a lifetime of oppression by fear. You *can* walk out the door without checking the electrical outlets a zillion times. You *can* leave the confines of your house and experience what's out there. You *can* walk on dirt with your bare feet. You *don't* have to wash your hands a gazillion times a day. You *don't* have to repeat yourself over and over. You *can* handle a normal number of loads of laundry like other people instead of washing clothes and bedding unnecessarily. You *can* have healthy relationships with your family and friends. You *don't* have to choose your words perfectly; no one does.

When you feel like your world is falling down all around you, when it feels like a tornado of the soul has just blown your life to smithereens, when you have such depth of sorrow and despair that you struggle with going forward, God promises to build your life up again with a rock-solid foundation. He promises you a life of that which is beautiful, radiant, and priceless—one that may seem hard for you to imagine in light of your present circumstances. He loves us so much that He goes beyond *our* welfare and ensures the welfare of our children and grandchildren; He cares about *all* that which concerns us. The establishment of our lives is of Him. Oppression and terror will not be part of our lives. If we find ourselves under attack, it will not last. When the dust has settled, you will come out on top. False accusation will fall by the wayside. God is your great Defender and Vindicator (Isaiah 54:11–17).

CHAPTER 7

Specific Areas of Concern

Subtitles

Anxiety
Fear
Unhealthy Thinking
Am I Crazy?
I Feel So Alone
Indecisiveness
Condemnation
Bad Consequences of My Words and Actions
My Life Is Such a Mess
I'll Never Get Better
Unnecessary Apologies
Mentally Rehashing Conversations
Perfectionism / Perfectionist Speech
Literal Speaking and Listening
Legalism
Negative Opinions of Others
I'm So Tired

Why Is This Happening to Me?
Counting
Clutter/Hoarding, a.k.a. "Stuff"
Paper Clutter
Shopping / Garage Sales
Skewed Sense of Balance
Unrealistic Concept of Time
Failure to Set Goals and Plan
Procrastination
Easily Sidetracked
Obsessing on Religion/God
Compulsive Behavior

Anxiety

Praying Scripture back to God is one way of dealing with anxiety. When I say "pray Scripture," I mean literally to pray God's Word back to Him. For example, let's say you are dealing with a situation, and you feel yourself becoming anxious. You can say, "God, You say, 'Be anxious for nothing, but in everything by prayer and supplication with thanksgiving let your requests be made known to God. And the peace of God, which surpasses all comprehension, shall guard your hearts and your minds in Christ Jesus.' (Philippians 4:6–7). So, Lord, I ask that You help me not to be anxious. I ask that You help me to deal with this situation in a manner that is pleasing to You and help me to face it unafraid. Thank You, Lord, that You are with me and helping me, and thank You, Lord, that You are helping me to grow. In Jesus's name I pray. Amen."

Some other helpful verses are Psalm 46:10 and 1 Peter 5:7. Psalm 46:10 is good when you find yourself all riled up about something. This verse reminds us that God knows all of the details, and *He* is on His throne. First Peter 5:7 reminds us how much God loves us and that we don't have to carry our troubles around with us. He's got your back.

God does not want our hearts to be weighed down with worry, anxiety, and troubles. Our hearts were not made to carry burdens. Our worrying, fretting, and anxiety do not fix anything; in fact, they add to the problem. God wants our hearts to be light, full of life, and carefree; He wants us to believe just how much He loves us and that He is there to take most excellent care of us (John 14:1). He desires prosperity for us in every way, most specifically in every dimension of our very beings (3 John 2).

Fear

Fear hinders us from living. Sometimes, it stops us dead in our tracks and can cause us to camp out along the roadway of life and delay us from reaching our destination. It may even cause some not only to forsake the way to fulfillment of their purposes in life but to also turn around and go back. Fear can catch us unaware. It is a deadly enemy of our souls! It keeps us focused on the bad and the hurtful, some of which never comes to pass anyway, instead of living life to the full in the present and looking and planning for the future with excitement and joyful anticipation.

There are numerous verses in the Bible relating to fear. This is *very* pertinent when dealing with OCD. Following are some Scripture references.

When you don't know which way to turn and all seems dark, God will be your light. In the midst of any circumstance with which you may be dealing, He will be there to save you. You can face your problems boldly; you don't need to succumb to fear and dread. He is our great defender no matter who or what or how much opposition may be coming against us. We will sense a holy confidence rising within us (Psalm 27:1–3).

In the midst of any storm, you can seek shelter in Him. When your strength is waning, He will give you His. Even when we think that it is *our* strength, any strength that we *do* have originated from Him. No matter the trouble, He will be right there with you to help; you're not doing this alone. In Him, fear will not triumph (Psalm 46:1–2).

God doesn't want us in bondage to anything. Bondage and fear are walking partners. Those who accept and embrace Him, the God of the universe adopts as His very own. He is the absolute best Daddy there is! (Romans 8:15).

If we find ourselves continually living in fear, we need to know this mind-set did not come from God. We are destined to live confidently and boldly, walking in a peaceful and beneficial love, realizing that we need not be tormented in our minds (2 Timothy 1:7 KJV).

Resist being controlled by fear, and choose God and His ways for you instead. You do not need to live in a state of constant fear. This is not of God. God is a God of life, *Zoe* (Greek) life, life to the fullest! Start living!

Unhealthy Thinking

Little children tend to be carefree; they don't know about germs. They are dependent upon others for their well-being while they eat, sleep, and play. As they grow, they are taught how to take care of themselves. The child who used to play in the dirt, wet his pants, and eat candy that had fallen onto the floor now learns to wash his hands when they get dirty and *not* to eat food that has fallen onto the floor.

If a person is not careful, he or she can get hung up on normal hygiene rules and go *beyond* the norm, resulting in obsessive-compulsive behavior. However, the focus of your thoughts need *not* be on the negative factor that is the driving force behind the obsessive-compulsive behavior but on the answer, solution, truth, and remedy to the concern that drives the unhealthy behavior. God encourages us to pay attention to everything that we are thinking about. What we think about truly makes a difference!

> *We are* destroying speculations and every lofty thing raised up against the knowledge of God, and *we are* taking every thought captive to the obedience of Christ. (2 Corinthians 10:5)

God gives us the power to control what we are thinking. Isn't that an awesome concept?

Pay attention to your thought life. What are you thinking about? Does it line up with God's Word? You will need to know what is *in* God's Word in order to know if your thoughts line up with that Word. Philippians 4:8 tells us where our focus is to be:

> Finally, brethren,
> whatever is true,
> whatever is honorable,
> whatever is right,
> whatever is pure,
> whatever is lovely,
> whatever is of good repute,
> if there is any excellence
> and if anything worthy of praise,
> let your mind dwell on these things.

Let this verse be a guide to see if your thought life is on track. Let it be a litmus test to determine whether your thoughts are lining up with true living. You don't have to be weighed down by bad, negative, and worrisome thoughts.

Am I Crazy?

Obsessive-compulsive disorder is very wearing on the mind. You might find yourself thinking, *What's wrong with me? Am I crazy?* If you are a Christian, I can assure you you're not crazy! Satan would like you to *think* that you are, but you are not (2 Timothy 1:7 KJV). Your thinking may be messed up, but you're *not* crazy.

As God reveals truth to us and we adjust our thinking in accordance with that truth, our faulty thought patterns will be corrected, and a transformation will take place in us. The new thought patterns will be good and life-producing (Romans 12:2).

Take the focus off of yourself, and put it onto God. As a Christian, know that Christ has you hidden in the safest place there is. When God looks at you, He sees His Son, Jesus (Colossians 3:3; Psalm 32:7; Psalm 119:114).

Before I had a name for what was going on in my thought life, words, and actions, I counseled with a pastor for a period of time, but he wasn't able to get to the bottom of what was going on with me. At that time, there was not as much awareness of OCD as there is now. So from there, I went for professional counseling. I even worried about what I told the counselor. There, too, the counselor did not talk to me about OCD.

It was frustrating not totally knowing why I behaved the way that I did yet realizing that something wasn't right. I wanted to change. I didn't want to stay the way that I was. Once you can *identify* what you are dealing with, it is easier to confront it. Truth is liberating (John 8:32).

Sometimes, it's comforting to know that we're not the only one going through something. It helps assure us that our situation is not as strange as it may seem and conjointly that we are not as weird as we or others may think (1 Corinthians 10:13). You are not alone in your ordeal. Many, many people have experienced the same goofy thoughts and behavior that you have, but God will not leave you there. The words in this book are written to give you hope and to assure you that by God's grace, you will not remain this way.

I Feel So Alone

When no other person is in your presence, it *appears* that you are alone. However, God is everywhere. There is no place that you can be that God's Spirit will not be there. He will always be there no matter where we run or fly. Whether it be the glorious heights of heaven above or the bottom of the ocean depths, God's Spirit will be there to lead. He is always available to come to our aid (Psalm 139:7–10).

If you are a Christian, God's very Spirit is resident *within* your body. Our bodies are intended to be His temple (1 Corinthians 3:16). His Spirit is available to us to help, comfort, guide, and instruct. We are never alone.

Jesus told His disciples that He would request that God His Father give the Holy Spirit to help them so that they would never be alone. The Holy Spirit speaks only truth. Only those who know God will be able to receive the Holy Spirit to live within them. Jesus knew that He would be leaving this earth before long, and He assured His friends that they weren't going to be left on their own. Even though Jesus's friends would no longer be able to seek Him out as they had been accustomed to doing, they would still be able to communicate with Him through His Spirit. Because of Him, they would truly live. God and His followers would be inseparable (John 14:16–20).

Learn to do what I call "practicing His presence." Choose to remind yourself that God is with you. Because He is omnipresent, remind yourself that He is with you *outwardly* (outside of your body). During your prayer time, imagine that God is sitting in a chair in the room with you. As a Christian, remind yourself especially of the fact that He is with you *inwardly.*

Be bold. He will give you what you need to do this thing. You don't need to be afraid all of the time, and you don't need to be shakin' in your boots; God Almighty is on your side. He is trustworthy and will never leave you to fend for yourself (Deuteronomy 31:6). Believe what you cannot see; more important, believe in *Whom* you cannot see (2 Corinthians 5:7). God is the saint's biggest fan and advocate. No matter who or what may seem to be coming against you, He is also your biggest cheerleader (Romans 8:31).

Indecisiveness

Sometimes, you might find yourself in a situation where you need to make a decision, and you are uncertain which way to go. If time permits, pray and then wait and see what God leads you to do. If time warrants a decision *now*, go with the answer that brings the most *peace* inside of you. Your *head* may not understand it, and it may even seem to your *mind* that you are making the wrong decision in conjunction with the facts that your head knows. However, God knows everything, especially the things that you don't know.

You may have more peace about accepting the job offer that accompanies less pay, and this does not make sense to your head. Maybe you will find more personal satisfaction at this company. Maybe you will be promoted and earn even more than what the other company is presently offering. Maybe in time you will buy a franchise or purchase the company.

Lack of peace in reaching a decision could be attributed to a myriad of possibilities known only to God. Maybe the company will fold in six months. Maybe your superior would have unethical work practices, or maybe your job would somehow jeopardize your marriage. Peace from God is meant to govern; lack of His peace is a big red flag (Colossians 3:15). It's like a close call at a ball game; the referee is the one who makes the call. In our lives, the Spirit of God residing inside of us will make the call as to what we are to do and not do. Heed His peace or lack thereof. Jesus is the Prince of Peace:

> For unto us a child is born, unto us a son is given: and the government shall be upon his shoulder: and his name shall be called Wonderful, Counsellor, The mighty God, The everlasting Father, The Prince of Peace. (Isaiah 9:6 KJV)

You may even be about ready to go out the door or do something or say something, and you sense a lack of peace about what you are about to do. Don't do it. Learn to be sensitive to God's Spirit within you.

Condemnation

When dealing with OCD, I suspect it common to deal with feelings of condemnation because of the numerous times that we've messed up. Quite often, after manifesting obsessive-compulsive disorder behavior, we realize that we didn't need to do or say whatever it is that we just did or said; sometimes, we realize it right away. You might be tempted to beat yourself up over it. Don't! God doesn't want you living under any condemnation! (Romans 8:1). "For God sent not his Son into the world to condemn the world; but that the world through him might be saved" (John 3:17 KJV).

God wants us to live healthily. He wants us to be sound in our thinking and behavior. If we're *doing it wrong*, He wants us to change, but He does *not* want us to live under condemnation from Satan, others, or even ourselves. The very One who made us is on our side (Psalm 56:9). God is not against us. Even when we *do* mess up, He's got our back; who is going to argue with Him about that? Jesus died in our place so that we don't have to experience fully what our sins rightly deserve. On top of that, He talks to His Father on our behalf. Wow! (Romans 8:33–34).

Bad Consequences of My Words and Actions

Just because those who are born again are not under condemnation does not mean that they will not suffer *consequences* for their messed-up behavior in regards to OCD. If we behave goofily, we're going to get unpleasant results; our lives will be negatively affected, as well as our relationships with God and others.

God does not want us to experience this kind of suffering. He doesn't want us to suffer needlessly (1 Peter 3:17). This type of suffering can be prevented by making wise and healthy choices that result in a wise and healthy life. Our words and actions of today are big determining factors of our future tomorrows (Galatians 6:7).

Whenever you realize that you have just done "something goofy," talk to God about it. If you've experienced the forgiveness of your sins, thank God that He has already forgiven you, and ask Him to help you do better in this area. Be obedient to whatever God may lead you to do or not do in regard to the offense.

Don't ever think that you have to address the problem on your own. Lean on God. Let Him help you. It is His heart's desire to be there for you (John 14:26). Over and over again in the Old Testament, there are examples of God's love expressed to His people as they repented of sin. As it says twenty-six times in Psalm 136, "For His lovingkindness is everlasting." Hallelujah!

But it gets even better! Read on!

My Life Is Such a Mess

You may be thinking that your life is such a mess and that it's been that way for a long, long time. You've tried and tried and tried, and you're not sure what to do. Discouragement and hopelessness may be staring you in the face. I want to encourage you and give you hope.

As born-again children of God, not only do we have available the love, forgiveness, grace, mercy, and help and the presence of God Himself in the person of His Holy Spirit, but we have the assurance that He will bring good out of any and all situations, including the bad circumstances of our lives (Romans 8:28). What an awesome promise! He promises to take each and every one of our failures, no matter how big or small, and cause them to benefit us. Who but God could do this? This also includes all of the bad things that have happened *to us* through no fault of our own; some have been pretty bad. This also includes everything that has happened every- and anywhere. Wow! We understand easily the thought that good proceeds from good, but God takes it all and does something marvelous with it! What an awesome God!

No matter what it may be, God's got it covered. No matter what we're facing, as long as He is welcome in the picture, He says, "I've got it. I know what to do. Turn the page. Keep reading." We don't have to rewrite our lives or scrap Chapters 5 through 9. What we would pitch, He redeems. He's the Master Scriptwriter of all time. No one can top Him or stop Him or have better creative ideas than He has.

It's kind of like baking a cake. Some of the ingredients, on their own, would not be very appealing to the taste—a raw egg, slippery vegetable oil, salt, baking powder, and dry flour. Some would taste good—sugar, apples, cherries, nuts, and pudding. But apply heat to all of the ingredients mixed together in the right proportions, and you end up with something that is very desirable to the taste.

So no matter where you are, what you have done, or what has been done to you, God can make it beautiful. The greater the challenge, the more jubilant the victory. Your story isn't finished. It has a happy ending. What a promise!

He hath made every *thing* beautiful in his time: …
—Ecclesiastes 3:11 (KJV)

I'll Never Get Better

Don't get stuck in the mentality "I'll always be this way; I'll never change." Even if you have been diagnosed medically as having OCD, don't allow it to be ingrained in your mind that you will always have OCD. There is hope. The God who created you is the Great Physician.

All throughout the Bible are examples of people with distorted pasts who by contact with the living God were forever changed. Mary, a woman of bad reputation, is mentioned in Luke 7:36–50. Although she had a sinful past, the love of Jesus ministered to her heart and her deepest needs, needs that no person could meet but God Himself, and she would never be the same. She was so transformed that Jesus Himself publicly defended her, not her sins, at the Pharisee's house.

Just as the love of Jesus transformed Mary, His love will do so for you as you have a personal encounter with Him. As we continue to follow Jesus and heed His voice, making wise decisions big and small on a consistent, daily basis, we and our lives will improve with each passing day. Gradually, as time goes on, we will be able to look back and not only *say* but *recognize* that we are no longer the people we used to be. A transformation will have taken place by the power of His Spirit. Our lives continue to be more and more glorious (2 Corinthians 3:18).

You can start out a sinner and end up a saint, and you don't have to wait until you die; there are saints living upon the earth today. One is qualified to be called a *saint* according to the Word of God. In the New Testament, "saints" is the title given to those who know and follow Jesus (Romans 1:7; 1 Corinthians 1:2).

So forsake the self-image of chopped liver, and rise up, O child of God! Look into the Word of God, and see yourself the way your heavenly Father sees you. We can look through the lens of a Father's love for us. We may not fully comprehend it in this lifetime, but we can embrace what His Word and His Spirit are telling us (1 Corinthians 13:12).

Unnecessary Apologies

Be careful *not* to fall into the trap of apologizing excessively. By "excessively" I do not necessarily mean apologizing repeatedly in the same conversation for the same incident over and over again, although that is not good also. What I mean by "excessively" is if you have fallen into the trap of habitually apologizing for a multitude of reasons and find yourself apologizing every time you turn around; others may have even brought this to your attention.

Do not apologize unnecessarily. Even if you have committed an offense with your mouth, it may not warrant an apology directly to the person with whom you were speaking. You don't have to voice your every thought. Don't waste your and others' time and energy on unnecessary apologies.

As you grow in God, you learn to recognize His voice and the leading of His Holy Spirit. Be sensitive to His voice, leading, and promptings, and follow His lead. Even Jesus did not do things completely of His own accord. He spoke what He learned from His Father (John 8:28).

Extend the same kind of grace and mercy to *yourself* that you show to others. Just as you wouldn't want your friends apologizing to you for every little thing, realize that they don't expect that of you either. Relax. As you love the people in your life, don't forget to love yourself! (Matthew 19:19).

Mentally Rehashing Conversations

This one is *big*! It has probably been one of the most agonizing aspects of OCD for me. It can rob you of truly living life! I was *so* conscious of not wanting to tell a lie, not wanting to ruin someone's reputation, not wanting to sin, and not wanting to go to hell that I got into the horrible pattern of mentally rehashing conversations in my head. Don't do it! I'm not saying that you can never give thought to what you said; what I *am* talking about is the habitual pattern, day in and day out. If you are caught in this trap, you know what I am talking about. God does not want you under bondage where you feel the need to go over everything you say and do with a fine-tooth comb.

But there is hope. Our Creator desires us to know freedom in every area of our lives (Luke 4:18). Seek truth, and God will give you the truth that you need in order to experience release from this bad habit. You don't have to stay stuck in this horrible pattern. Mentally rehashing conversations is emotionally draining and mentally tiring. It is time-consuming. It takes you away from the present and attempts to draw you back into the past. As we proceed in pursuit of our life's endeavors, we are to look ahead as we move forward in life, not continually look backward.

> But Jesus said to him, "No one, after putting his hand to the plow and looking back, is fit for the kingdom of God."
> —Luke 9:62

I used to feel condemned when I would read this verse. Remember, if you are a born-again child of God, you are not under condemnation (Romans 8:1). Instead, let this verse (Luke 9:62) encourage you to leave the past behind, live in the present, and keep looking forward.

By continually going over conversations in your head, if you look hard enough and long enough, chances are you *are* going to find something that you're going to question whether you did it right or not. None of us are perfect; allow yourself to be human. Cut yourself some slack. There are many areas where we mess up. When it comes to *what* we say, *how* we say it, *when* we say it, and even *why* we say it, we all blow it at times. Jesus is the only One who has never said the wrong thing (James 3:2).

Perfectionism / Perfectionist Speech

I have dealt with perfectionism for years. It has been therapeutic for me to the extent that my eyes are being opened to see that many besides me do not have it all together; actually, no one does. The *appearance* of perfect does not equate to perfect. I guess I was kind of judging a book by its cover—I had a tendency to assume, to the degree that someone had the *appearance* of looking like he or she had it together, that it was so. Awareness that I am not so alone in dealing with life's issues encourages me—I'm not as strange of a duck as I thought.

Depending upon the circumstances, perfectionism can be an asset or a detriment. If time is of the essence, perfectionism can be a detriment. If it's a homemade craft or needlework, perfectionism can be an asset; it makes for a beautiful finished piece of work. Perfectionism can lend itself well to establishing the reputation for yourself and your trade. However, perfectionism can be a detriment when it comes to speech. Just as a person can be too loose with his or her lips, one can also be too precise. You can go too far in either direction (Proverbs 4:27).

Jesus tells us, "Therefore you are to be perfect, as your heavenly Father is perfect" (Matthew 5:48).

At times, I might have had an incorrect interpretation of what this verse meant in terms of being perfect. "*Be perfect*" in the aforementioned verse comes from the Greek word *Teleios*. My Bible's lexical aid has quite a lengthy definition. However, toward the end, it partially states,

> In Js. 1:4, "that you may be perfect" means that you may not be morally lacking. It has similar meaning in Mt. 5:48; … *Teleios* is not to be confused with *anamartetos*, without sin or sinless (361). (*The Hebrew-Greek Key Study Bible*, New American Standard, Lexical Aids to the New Testament)

Always strive to be better and to come up higher, but be realistic in your expectations. As long as you are on earth, you will probably err with your tongue. I say this not to discourage or even to speak fault with the tongue into your life, but I say it to spare you the awkwardness of trying too hard to speak without fault. It's not only a striving work for you, but the resulting choice of words can sound strange to others and even to yourself!

Attempt to minimize phrases that express question of doubt when the *motivation* behind choosing these particular words is to cover your tracks because you are so afraid of making a mistake in your speech. Examples of such phrases are "I'm not sure, but …" and "It was something like this." We always want to have *healthy* motives behind everything that we think, say, and do (Proverbs 16:2).

Trust that the Holy Spirit within you will help you to remember those things that you have said that you need to pay heed to. Conversely, don't get all hung up on what you *omitted* to say. Oh, how the devil loves to come at us with any angle that he can! If you have erred in any way in your speech and need to make it right, the Holy Spirit will let you know (John 14:26).

It's always good to pray *before* something instead of worrying about it *after* the fact. Don't falsely, naturally assume that just because you have the mental and physical capabilities that you can just get up in the morning and *do* this thing called *life* independent of being connected to God. Some good Scriptures to pray before we speak and at the start of every day are Psalm 19:14 and Psalm

141:3. One verse covers not only the mouth and the words that come out of it but also the thoughts behind those words. The other verse likewise addresses the mouth but also includes the element of helping us to keep our mouths shut, and who hasn't said something just to later regret saying it? Our jaw is like the hinges of a door. If only we would just keep that door shut at times—ah, yes. Both verses are directed *to* God and call upon Him directly for help in the area of our speech.

If perfectionism of speech is a challenging area in your life, relax more when it comes to conversation; it doesn't have to be hard. Sometimes we make life harder than what it needs to be—harder than what *God* intended it to be. Don't get so caught up in the precise wording of how you speak. It may take time, but the more you practice this, the more natural it will become. He wants you to walk and live your life freely and to rest in Him. If you're finding that life is too much of an uphill struggle, take it to God. Something's amiss. He'll help you figure it out (Matthew 11:28–30).

Sometimes, the best answer is for us to simply be quiet and let Him take care of it.

> Be still, and know that I *am* God: …
> —Psalm 46:10 (KJV)

Literal Speaking and Listening

Over time, I have come to realize that quite often I have been a *literal* speaker as well as listener. By "literal speaker and listener," I mean that I have had a bent to lean heavily upon the actual wording of what is being said and less upon other aspects of communication. This could be due to a combination of reasons, some of which are perfectionism, legalism, scrupulosity of speech, and transparency of heart.

Literal speaking and listening can be beneficial when details are important, such as when balancing a checkbook, doing counted cross-stitch, designing architectural drawings, and dispensing medication. However, it can be a problem when it comes to *relational* issues. Left to *literal* speaking and listening alone, one can miss elements pertinent to the topic or people at hand.

Recognize that when you say "a couple," *you* may mean *two*. Realize that someone else saying "a couple" may mean *three* or *four*. If the subject is discrepancy in a bank statement, the meaning will probably be *two*. If it's a matter of how many pieces of candy someone just ate, it could be *two*, three, or even *four*. People's style of communication varies. Some are more precise; others are less. Some tend to exaggerate or embellish more than others.

Because I have had the tendency to interpret conversations so literally, I would at times speak up more frequently than what was probably necessary and correct others' statements. Just as I was careful of my *own* speaking, I was also conscious of what *others* were saying while in my presence. This was partially attributed to the standpoint of a sense of obligation on my part—obligation to speak up in the event I thought an incorrect statement had been made. At times, this *is* appropriate. However, for someone dealing with OCD, there are times when this is not necessary. Learn to distinguish the difference. Discern which matters are weightier.

Certainly be aware of the other obvious forms of communication, such as body language, facial expression, and tone and inflection of voice, but also the not so obvious. Learn to read between the lines without being presumptuous. Recognize what is *not* being said.

Although *you* may have a tendency to tell it like it is, not all people may be as forthright. You might ask a friend if she wants to go see a particular movie. She replies, "What do you want to go see *that* movie for?" Unbeknown to you, she does not want to go see the movie but does not want to tell you "no." So instead of answering your question directly, she circumvents doing so and directs the conversation elsewhere. Unless you learn to recognize what's going on, you may think that she is truly asking a question to which you would give a reply, when she doesn't really want one anyway.

Also, recognize the difference between a genuine question and a rhetorical one. Some are more obvious than others for me. This particular issue has caught me by surprise, maybe in part because of English grammar education that implies that a question asks for an answer. For clarification for my understanding of the conversation at hand, sometimes I will ask outright if the person wants an answer or if he or she is making a statement. Some people use rhetorical questions as a *regular* form of communicating *statements*; this can be confusing to me. By recognizing what is transpiring on the part of both parties, I can adjust *my* way of communicating.

Be mindful of not living by the letter but by being sensitive to the Spirit of God within you. The first style results in trouble; the latter is life-producing (2 Corinthians 3:6). Don't get hung up on the *words* that are being spoken, but instead think to pay attention to what the Holy Spirit may be telling you. Jesus said, "I am come that they might have life, and that they might have *it* more abundantly" (John 10:10 KJV).

Legalism

This area was *huge* in my life! I touched upon this in chapters 1 and 3. Much of what I have already written could be filed as subsets of legalism or be interwoven with it, but because of the role that legalism played in my life, I want to draw attention to this issue specifically. It is imperative that this issue be recognized and dealt with when it is present in an individual's life. Because of the importance of this issue, God personally addressed it in the book of Romans.

Legalism is a killer. It will suck the life out of you! Don't go this route! Legalism is when you are trying to live your life by formula—a list of dos and don'ts, while God and people are secondary or nonexistent in your life. Life doesn't work this way. If this has been your approach to life, you may be getting by, but sooner or later, the brokenness resulting from this lifestyle will appear. If nothing else, legalism takes a huge toll on the individual who approaches life with this mind-set.

Presently, God is taking me to a deeper level of understanding in this area. I may not yet fully comprehend the degree to which this mental list of dos and don'ts, in addition to a perfectionist viewpoint, have negatively affected my mind-set and way of living, but I am thankful God continues to reveal truth to me—truth that I need to correct faulty thinking patterns.

It's like I subconsciously had formed this idea that *living by this list of dos and don'ts + everybody "doing" it right (perfectionism) =* a good life for everybody. In a sense, it would be nice if life *did* fit into a formula. Life would be more predictable; others would do more accordingly to what we expect them to do and vice versa. The only way that this would be able to happen is if we were to be like robots, everybody doing A, B, and C in the proper order and at the proper time—that is, A + B = C—but that isn't how real life is, neither is it how God operates in our lives. We're not little creatures of a video game that He is playing. He doesn't *force* us to do anything. He *wants* us to do what's right and good, especially because He knows that we will benefit thereby, and He certainly does everything in His power to lead us in the right direction. But we are *not* robots, and real life isn't pigeon-holed into a formula—man's formula anyway. The only formula that works is *God's* formula.

Life, true life, is all about relationship—relationship with God our Creator and relationship with one another. When we try to do either of these relationships by formula, a list of dos and don'ts, a checklist, we get into trouble. Imagine what it would be like if you approached relationship with your spouse or children by a mental checklist. That is what it's like when we try to approach God by the method of attempting to be good enough but never truly sharing *ourselves* with Him. Just like the love-starved wife who desires her husband's attention and affection, she tells him that it's not about the money, house, cars, or trip to Jamaica. Just as her heart longs for *him*, God desires *us*. The key to loosing the chains of legalism is wrapped up in a one-on-one relationship with Jesus. The very Creator of the universe created us, because He desired for us to be, and He desired to have an ongoing relationship with each and every one of us.

> Therefore the Law has become our tutor *to lead us* to Christ, that we may be justified by faith.
> —Galatians 3:24

Negative Opinions of Others

Positive advice and constructive criticism are good for maturity. The person who is able to reprove in accordance with wisdom is like a piece of fine jewelry to the ear that is receptive (Proverbs 25:12). A man of understanding will benefit from such reproof (Proverbs 19:25).

It would be best if such correction came wrapped in love and grace and mercy, but it doesn't always happen that way. Sometimes, it's overlaid with shame and condescension. Even then we can benefit from such criticism. At minimum, you can take it to God in prayer. Maybe you have a fault that you are well aware of, or maybe it's something that you never even thought of before. Either way, He knows us as we are, better than we even know ourselves.

When others attempt to use shame to bring us around, maybe they don't know a better way to do it, or maybe that's how they were taught. I believe they have good intentions, albeit not the best methods. Learn to differentiate the *truth* of the matter from the *method* of communicating that truth. Even though you might have felt unloved, shamed, and devalued, glean the truth and discard the negative. Choose to refuse to be offended and be determined to grow from the experience.

Do not base your self-esteem on the negative words and opinions of others. Base the opinions of yourself on what *God* says about you in His Word. His Word trumps the opinions of others every time. Realize that someone may have a bad opinion of you, but their opinion does not necessarily equate with truth. Learn to grow above the concept that I'm no good unless others validate me; that concept may be valid in the world's system, but it does not hold water in God's kingdom. Learn to think and live above the world's viewpoint of life and begin to operate in the ways of God's kingdom, which is unseen to the natural eye.

Jesus, our very Creator, King of the universe, God Himself, knew what it was like to be misunderstood and devalued in the eyes of men. When He lived upon earth, many knew not the worth of Him. He knew what it was to be despised. People forsook the One who loved them the most. He knew personal sorrow; grief was no stranger to Him. People acted like they didn't want to be around Him. He wasn't seen for His true worth. An honorable burial He was not given, yet He was as innocent as a Lamb (Isaiah 53:3, 9).

Come to know that even if you were to have no one else, Jesus is there for you. Then you can withstand anything. If you are secure in God's great love for you, you will be able to weather any of the storms of life, even death itself because you are secure in the magnitude of every dimension of Christ's love (Ephesians 3:17–19).

Years ago, I was in a church, and we were singing a song with lyrics that expressed our need for God. We *do* need God, and we all need other *people*. God designed us to be relational—with Him and others. God knows our basic needs, and He guides us in the fulfillment of those needs. If for some reason a need is not being met, He will be there to meet that need or guide us to the meeting of that need. God is everything in life that we need Him to be. It's like He gives us a blank check for us to fill in, but instead of a dollar amount, the blank on the check beckons an identity of who God can be in our lives (Exodus 3:14).

In the Gospel of John, Jesus was preparing His disciples for His bodily departure from this earth. Thomas thought that he didn't know how to get to where Jesus was going, even though Jesus had already told Thomas that he did in fact know. Thomas's answer was standing right before his very eyes (John 14:2–6). Whatever you are in need of, look to Jesus. He is the best and closest friend that you will ever have (Proverbs 18:24).

If you are a person of tender heart and sensitive conscience, recognize that just because someone may respond harshly or negatively toward you does not necessarily mean that you are in the wrong!

I'm So Tired

You may find yourself thinking, *I'm so tired of being this way and living like this.* Even though you may not presently be where you want to be and are well aware of your own shortcomings, persevere (Philippians 3:12). Your race isn't over yet. Don't give up, and don't drop out. You haven't reached the finish line yet; you're in the *middle* of this thing. Keep on keeping on. You'll get it. Have a winner's mentality (1 Corinthians 9:24).

Don't keep thinking of all the times that you blew it; don't keep looking backward. Look straight ahead, and go forward. Focus on what you want your life to look like. Keep your goal in your mind's eye and ever before you (Philippians 3:13–14, Proverbs 4:25). It's more important how you *finish* your life than how you started your life, so don't get hung up on all the times that you fell down in between. The completion of a thing is more important than having started it (Ecclesiastes 7:8).

Don't allow your focus to be on the past and your failures and shortcomings of that time. You are not doomed to the patterns, mistakes, or history of your yesterdays. You are not even bound by the circumstances of the present. Sometimes *we* are the ones who allow our sins to be kept before our eyes; God is the one who continually gives us a clean slate day by day (Psalm 103:12). Our God is a God of freedom—freedom to live the great lives that we envision (John 8:36).

What is important is today and tomorrow and every decision we make henceforth. We live in the present, walking into our future. God's salvation is available to us now. He helps us to make wise and healthy choices (2 Corinthians 6:2). Today, we can choose salvation in Jesus Christ and make a fresh start. Every day that we open our eyes to live one more day, we can choose afresh. God makes everything new (Revelation 21:5).

Be mindful of these things, and you will remain hopeful—the well of God's golden supply of lovingkindness never runs dry. Even when others lose patience with us or we are short with them, God's compassion is a constant commodity. Any day of the week, He replenishes a fresh supply, ever new. He is the most faithful, true-blue Friend that you could and will ever have! He is faithful to be there always with whatever you have need of (Lamentations 3:21–23).

Never give up hope; it is there for the asking (1 Corinthians 13:13). If you are lacking in hope, ask Father God to give you hope. He promises to give to those who ask. As you ask, you will receive. Just as we as earthly parents do not hurt our children by intentionally giving them something bad when they have asked of us something good, likewise our heavenly Father loves to hear from His children, and He loves to not only meet their needs but He also loves to bless them with the most awesome and beautiful gifts. In fact, He goes beyond the way that we give (Matthew 7:7–11).

Continue keeping on, moving on, going forward, coming up higher, and growing in Him. You can do it. You're going to make it. You are able to do this thing. Trust God to give you strength (Philippians 4:13). When God starts a project, He completes it; He started something in you, and He's not going to drop it now (Philippians 1:6).

Recognize that there are going to be hurdles along the way; just don't allow those hurdles to be permanent roadblocks to your success. Endurance is the necessary commodity at this time to help you complete this thing and finish strong. Pay attention to where your focus is. Look to Jesus, who gave you the faith to start. By focusing on the joy that lay ahead, He was able to endure much suffering and shame. Because of His singular focus and faithfulness, He now holds a position of highest honor. Remember Him as an example from which to draw encouragement when you're feeling tired (Hebrews 12:1–3).

Why Is This Happening to Me?

Although dealing with obsessive-compulsive disorder can be very painful and frustrating, it *can* be overcome, and there is a flip side to this intrusive dilemma. As a result of going through the trial of living with OCD and coming out at the other end victorious, people are able to help others who may be dealing with OCD in the present.

Whatever affliction you are going through, others will be comforted and encouraged through your experience (2 Corinthians 1:6). People will listen to what you have to say, because you understand and have walked in their shoes. God is a good Father! He is merciful and comforts His children. He does this not only out of His love for us but because He wants us to pass this same comfort on to others who need it just like we did (2 Corinthians 1:3–4).

Just as God has comforted me, I pass that same comfort on to you! Think of it. How many times have you been comforted or encouraged because you ended up talking with someone who was dealing with similar circumstances as you were or had already been through it? You were encouraged, helped, or comforted, because you could tell that they understood just what you were going through. I hope that the words of this book are a medicinal salve to your emotional wounds and that these words will speak to your circumstances such that they will reveal truth that will lead to freedom!

Many times, we don't know why we are going through whatever it is that seems to be so monumental, oppressive, and life-draining. Sometimes, we don't understand until we come out at the other end.

The story of Joseph in the book of Genesis is an example of someone who endured terrible injustice at the hands of his brothers, the very ones who should have been counted among the most trustworthy. Although Joseph had been done a terrible wrong and can rightly be portrayed as a victim, he didn't allow himself to stay in the victim mentality. In the end, not only Joseph's brothers but his entire family would benefit from his station in life. He truly rose above his circumstances instead of allowing himself to be overcome by them (Deuteronomy 28:13). In the natural, it looked like he was defeated in the midst of all of his troubles, but God had a plan for his life that was bigger than the plan to defeat it.

Do not abandon hope. Hang in there, persevere, and keep praying and seeking God and His answers. In the end, you will find yourself in the position of Joseph, who saw God's hand in the circumstances. To your surprise, what presently seems so disproportionately weighted on the side of injustice or pain in the end will reveal the greater good that God had planned all along (Genesis 50:20).

Pay attention to where your focus is. Always keep Jesus center stage; He is the One who started your faith journey and the One who will continue to move in your life (Hebrews 12:2). If you focus and dwell on the negative, it will bring you down; it is too discouraging. It can be overwhelming. Jesus is your life (John 14:6). He's the One with all the answers.

Keep your eyes and ears open. When all is said and done, you will see that just as in the life of Joseph, the One who fashioned you and destined you to be will have caused every single bit of all that is bad to result in good on your behalf! (Romans 8:28).

Counting

Interesting—that is the word that comes to mind. Sometimes, I will find myself counting in my head.

The other day, I was washing dishes. As I was washing a glass, I realized that I was counting in my head as I was wiping the dishcloth around and over the edge of the circumference of the top of the glass. I was counting, "1, 2, 3, 4." *Why?*—I'm not exactly sure. Maybe I started the habit a long time ago? Maybe by mentally dividing the circumference of the glass into four sections and counting to four as I wash, I am determining that I have adequately washed the total rim?

Once while I was waiting at a medical office, I discovered that I was counting the ceiling tiles.

Could it have to do with whatever activity is going on in the brain in the area that deals with numbers? I liked math and did well in math classes—*what connection might this have?*

Most of the time, this "counting" does not seem to pose a significant issue. Lately, I have been learning time management. The thought *did* cross my mind whether I am doing too many swipes around the rim of the glass—smile and a chuckle. This ought to be interesting to find out.

Clutter/Hoarding, a.k.a. "Stuff"

The word *hoarding* in the title gets my attention. I have known for years that I have had a problem with *clutter* and that I had a bunch of *stuff*. Until recently, I had not given much thought to the idea that I might be a *hoarder*.

I had come to a certain level of acceptance regarding *clutter* and *stuff*—acceptance that I have a problem and am challenged in this area. To a degree, I have even experienced the feeling that I was a prisoner to my house, the things within it, and the unattended-to responsibilities represented there.

The word *hoarder*, however, carries a significantly different connotation than *clutter* and *stuff*, depending upon the level of hoarding, especially in light of reality television that addresses this topic. Some people may even be *organized* hoarders, and because of their organization skills, they may not be readily perceived as hoarders by themselves or others. Some of what I have seen on TV is not too pretty. I have appreciated watching such a show though because through real-life people, I can relate. I can see and hear myself and learn from what I am seeing and hearing.

I can also relate with the frustrated hoarders who did not seem to be as successful as others in their attempt to get rid of a ton of stuff and bring simplicity and order to their lives. Because of the dynamics in the thinking process that takes place in the mind of a hoarder, I suspect that I, too, would have a hard time parting with so much stuff on a large scale in such a condensed period of time.

It isn't always a matter of the obvious. To one person, the tattered dress over in the corner is well ready for the garbage. To another, it's a visual reminder of the dress that was borrowed before the dog got ahold of it. If it gets thrown out, one might forget all about it and never compensate the owner for the dress.

As I drive down the road, my eyes have gravitated to the items that have been set out by the side of the road for the garbage. This makes me smile just thinking about it. I realize not everybody does or would be interested in doing this. I am not above picking something up in this manner, although I do like the idea of asking the owner's permission. Some people will intentionally get rid of their stuff this way, knowing and expecting that somebody might come by and pick it up.

The forgetfulness factor has played into my life in the area of clutter. I have found that sometimes if it's out of sight, it's out of mind. That is why sometimes I have left things out in plain sight—so I don't forget about it. However, this method is not effective for pleasant surroundings.

Another factor that played into clutter is that I got into the habit of laying things where they didn't belong. The clothes that needed ironing would end up draped over the back of a chair. The basket of clean laundry would get dumped on the bed but might not get folded right away. The coat, purse, and shopping bag might have landed on a chair. After having my first baby, I recognized that my habits left clues for something similar to an archeological site; all someone had to do was go through my home and observe objects lying around the house to figure out what I had been doing.

Another habit that has played into the problem that I have had with clutter was leaving tools and electrical devices out or opened because I planned on resuming whatever activity later, for example,

- vacuum cleaner (I have been notorious with this one)
- sewing machine cabinet, open with items waiting to be sewn on top
- ironing board with the iron perched on top along with clothing waiting to be ironed

It's a good thing that the washing machine and dryer are stationary. Just imagine what I could do with those!

The same concept applies to other *things*:

- even the dust rag draped over the back of the dining room chair, because the rag was hardly used and wasn't dirty enough yet to be tossed into the hamper, plus the thought that maybe I would get to some more dusting later
- the newspaper that I hadn't finished reading
- the stash of papers strewn across the dining room table

One can pick up on the common thread of completing or tackling a task later. Many times, later didn't come, and I would go to bed with the items the way they were left, or there would be the quick exercise of transferring whatever was on top of the bed onto a chair. In the morning, I would start all over again, with the "stuff" awaiting me from where it had been laid the day before. As you can guess, many times, I did not necessarily resume where I had left off the day before, and the cycle would continue—adding clutter to more clutter.

This probably shouts disorganization, lack of self-discipline, and poor planning—all of which are probably true and applicable—but I don't believe these factors to be independent of others mentioned in this section and in other parts of the book.

People like me become desensitized to the chaos and disorganization around us. We get used to the pile of clothing on the living room chair, rationalizing it away in our mind. We can give you the excuses as to why we have not and are not tending to it at this time. We have shelved this task to a place in the back of our mind, to be addressed at a later time or day. For whatever reason, we don't think that we have time for this right now. Something or somebody else (could be ourselves) has priority for the time being. As time progresses, we move the thought of the visible to the back of our mind, thus coping with our surroundings.

The clutter *does* bother us, however, not only when it is

only *us* living among the clutter but especially when unexpected company shows up at the door. A cluttered home environment is *not* what we want. We don't deny that it bothers us. Maybe we don't recognize how we are truly "doing it wrong." Maybe we at times just feel overwhelmed and discouraged. Other times, it may seem like it's an ongoing battle—between us and the stuff. Maybe we're not sure of the game plan. Maybe there are truly other more imposing problems in our lives that sabotage our productivity.

I find it very interesting that just yesterday I was in the waiting lounge of a university hospital medical facility. Across from me was a stand that held various informational handouts available to the public. One paper was a golden yellow eight-and-a-half-by-eleven sheet of paper with the word *CLUTTER* in larger letters toward the top of the paper. As I sat there, the word *CLUTTER* caught my eye and attention. Upon skimming the information, I discovered that one could attend a number of appointments to apparently get help in dealing with the clutter in his or her life. Not only that, but insurance was sometimes applicable. Very interesting!

One area in which I have been *tempted* but haven't succumbed too much is in the context of my car and clutter. One could easily reinvent the purpose of the automobile to not only be a mode of transportation for people and their belongings—purse, school backpacks, grocery purchases, and so on—but also a mobile storage unit on wheels. I do *not* recommend this.

Clutter has its varied methods of multiplication. One is that of the reception of items bought or passed on by well-intentioned family or friends. Notice that I put the emphasis not on the *giving* but on the *reception*. It is *our* responsibility as to what finds a home within our homes. I am not saying that people should not buy us things or pass things down to us; I myself like knowing that my usable items have found a new home where someone will appreciate and use them. Be selective.

Paper Clutter

I have distinguished *paper clutter* as a *specific* subset of clutter because of the dimension that it has played in my life. It has weighed heavily upon me, kind of like a skeleton in my closet, except the closet door has been wide open at times. This particular area of challenge for me had such an—I don't know if I should say "negative" or "positive" (it's probably a mixture of both)—impact upon one of my daughters, that as a wife and mother of two little ones, in addition to being a full-time plus a part-time job worker, she has one of the most orderly homes that I know of. She is also one of the most organized people I know. It saddens me to know that my shortcomings in this area were a catalyst to her organization.

Although I am not able to give the "educated" response to the question of paper clutter, I *am* able to speak with the voice of experience. I do not even know if there is a documented link between paper clutter and obsessive-compulsive disorder, but I suspect there is. I *do* know that I have had and am currently dealing with a problem concerning paper. I believe a number of issues come into play:

Perfectionism—I want to do it right. I smile as I have written this. Sometimes, I have had the tendency to go over my paperwork with a fine-tooth comb. What if there is an error on the bill? Not only am I mindful of my *own* behavior, but I examine someone *else's* behavior, that is, how they handled my transactions and so on. I am not saying that you can't ever go over a bill to ensure that it is accurate, but if you deal with OCD, there may be times when you sense you are carrying things a bit too far.

Procrastination—This one has been a *huge* factor in my problem with papers. Sometimes, I have gotten the mail, gone into the house, laid the mail on the table or desk, and proceeded to do something different—started making dinner, got a load of laundry going, listened to the messages on the answering machine—with the intention of getting to the mail later. So often, later came untimely. Often, upon bringing the mail into the house, I wouldn't promptly discard the junk mail; I didn't even take the time to at minimum *open* the mail. One time, after my first husband died, I had a substantial check, waiting to be cashed, in one of my unopened pieces of mail!

I have even incurred late fees not because of lack of money but because of simply not paying the bill on time. I hate that! It's one thing to incur a late fee because you don't have the money; it's another to incur a late fee simply because of not getting around to it!

Don't want to miss anything—Interesting! Even the junk mail might have some coupons that I might want to use. What if there is an advertised function that I'm interested in? Information is valuable, but let's face it. There is a *lot* of information out there that never even reaches my mailbox, hands, eyes, or ears, and yet awareness of this fact does not weigh heavily upon me. Recently, I observed a gentleman standing by the side of the road, going through his mail and tossing items into the trash can. Now this is a goal that I would like to learn to emulate. The goal of having a clutter-free desk, dining room and kitchen tables, and countertops outweighs the risk of missing out on the trivial!

Lack of balance / Too much importance on the trivial—I know this is going to sound goofy, but do you remember the feeling you got the first time you received mail to your own address? First of all, it's an acknowledgment that you exist, that you're a person, even if it's junk mail. After all, if you didn't exist, you wouldn't be receiving it in the first place. Secondly, it makes me think that I have moved up, moved on, that I am independent; I'm receiving mail at my own address/receptacle. If I am dependent upon junk mail to make me feel important, I need to make some changes! This is not out of condemnation but realization.

Over-responsible—I want to handle my paperwork in a responsible fashion, but in my zeal to be responsible, I can actually end up *doing it wrong.* I do not have to read all of the fine print, all of the legal jargon on every piece of paper. I need to recognize that that is just what some of the print is—legal jargon and specifics to cover everything. If my telephone bill differs by twenty-five cents, do I really have to go over the bill to decipher why? If my bill is in the ballpark of the price it has been running, can't I just pay the bill and call it good? If I am on top of my paperwork and want to go over the bill to discern the discrepancy, fine, but if I am overcome with papers, I need to discern the important from the unimportant.

Hoarding / Piles of paper—Whether this is the applicable term or not, I do not know, but I suspect it applies. My filing system has been such that it's probable that at times I hold on to papers for too long or hold on to papers that I don't need to keep at all. Years ago, it was not uncommon for me to have piles of paper on my snack bar that faced the dining area. I used to tease that I shouldn't have anything that is *horizontal* in my house; the resulting piles of paper were part of the reason. As I write, I have piles of somewhat-alphabetized paper-clipped/clipped-together papers on my dining room table. Upon examining the items that *have been* filed, one might be able to discern that I like to organize. When I *do* it, I do it fairly well. What *doesn't* get organized is part of my problem.

Sticky notes—I would write lots of notes; if I didn't, sometimes I would forget things. Naturally, these notes contributed to my accumulation of paper. I had received a Palm Pilot as a Christmas gift, but it took me three years from the time that I had received it to start using it. Once I started using it, I discovered how much I benefited from its use. I now use my iPod; it is a tremendous help!

Overload of responsibility—I suspect this has come into play for me. I have willingly accepted that such and such was or would be my responsibility without proper consideration that just maybe I was trying to do too much and could benefit from a different distribution of responsibilities.

I have even caught myself voluntarily, maybe of my own

accord or initiation, taking on *additional* responsibility that was not mine. I'm precise, and I thought I would be helping. I perceived myself as maybe being better suited for the task than another person, and maybe because I didn't have an outside *job*, I thought I had the time to do it. Fortunately, I was told that I didn't need to be doing this particular chore, and I was relieved of the responsibility. However, it was not *I* who recognized the unhealthiness of what I was doing but someone else. I *have* grown, and, I hope, because I did eventually recognize the unhealthiness of what I had done, I will be less apt to repeat this type of behavior in the future.

Shopping / Garage Sales

I like garage sales; you can pick up some good bargains. Garage sales are great places to buy children's clothing and baby items. One of my best purchases was a used built-in dishwasher that I bought for five dollars from people who had remodeled their kitchen. The house in which I was living at the time had a built-in dishwasher, but it had not worked since the time we moved into the house. We needed to get two to three parts, and with the help of a plumber friend, a brother-in-law, and my husband, the garage-sale dishwasher was moved, installed, and up and running. It worked for years after that. Good deal!

Although I *did* acquire some good deals from garage sales, some of my purchases contributed to the growth of clutter in my home. Sometimes I would see something I liked, decide it was a good price, and buy it. After taking it home, I didn't always know where to put it. I still remember the black iron chandelier that I had purchased at a garage sale that ended up being stored in the basement and never *did* hang from a ceiling. There was the attractive antique-looking pink glass ceiling light bowl that also never found its intended purpose in my home.

Finally, I came to the recognition that it wasn't always good for me to go to garage sales. There was a period of time in which I was kind of staying away from them. Recently, I have been a garage-sale and thrift-store shopper, but I have to be careful.

There was even a time in my life that I sensed that God might have wanted me to curtail shopping. This went on for about a year. It isn't that I abstained altogether, but there *was* a difference—interesting.

Skewed Sense of Balance

Could it be that people who deal with OCD tendencies have a skewed sense of *balance*—in areas such as our acquisition of tangible things, piles of paper, perfectionism, speech, how we spend our time, and so on?

I observe in myself and have observed in others that we recognize the *value* and potential in many things. I am not referencing the *quantity* but the *usefulness* of something. The problem lies in a lack of a governor to bring us in balance. Thus, we get out of control, whether it is in our acquisition of things, clothing that overflows closet space, reusable plastic tubs, piles of paperwork awaiting our attention, or newspapers and magazines that have yet to be read.

Just the other day, I caught myself being tempted to save a clear plastic McDonald's glass with lid, realizing that it would serve as a good cup for future use. When I recognized my temptation, I resisted it and threw the cup away.

Our accustomed way of thinking needs to be balanced with correlating counterbalancing thoughts:

- Do I really need this?
- Is it worth the hassle?
- What about my time?

- What about the toll that the *sight* alone of the visible clutter takes on the emotional well-being of my family and me?
- Are my habits a source of tension or arguments?
- Am I on top of things, or am I always behind?
- What about the out-of-sight things that weigh on my subconscious?

The answers to these questions are not meant to condemn but to help shed light on the whole picture. The answers do not necessarily mean that we are all wrong and someone else is all right, but the answers can be clues to solving our dilemmas. By recognizing and putting a little more emphasis on the other part of the equation, our desired lives may be more easily attainable.

Don't be too quick to dismiss input from others; there could be more truth and wisdom in their words than we realize. Sometimes we get stuck in our own way of thinking and doing. Another's input might be our needed counterbalance. We may not always like what someone else may be telling us, but unbeknownst to us, it may be just what we need to hear. Their words might rub us the wrong way, but maybe it would be good to reconsider (Proverbs 27:17).

> See then that ye walk circumspectly, not as fools, but as wise.
> —Ephesians 5:15 (KJV)

Unrealistic Concept of Time

This is connected with the previous topic of a skewed sense of balance, but because of the significance of this issue, I am giving it selective attention. Just how much of a connection this particular topic has with OCD, I do not know, but if I have dealt with it, I suspect others who have wrestled with OCD have dealt with this, too.

Lately, I had asked God to teach me time management. I have had an unrealistic viewpoint concerning time. I wonder if having been a stay-at-home mom factored into this for me. Partly due to a lack of time constraints, I have had the tendency to think that I have more time than what I actually do. Because of this unrealistic thinking, I have used up more time doing something than what is practical. We do *not* have all the time in the world.

In determining whose responsibility it is to do a specific chore, there is also the related thought (whether it be yours or someone else's) that *you* should be able to do the chore, because it appears or is assumed that you have the time because of the fact that you don't have a regular job outside of the home. Recognize that you have chosen *not* to hold down a job outside of the home for whatever reasons. Are you fulfilling those objectives behind that decision, or are you getting bogged down in other things?

Sometimes, we are involved in too many activities. We may actually *like* some of these activities but fail to recognize our limitations of time and energy. We need to be selective and prioritize in order of importance and be willing to step back from some things.

Another hindrance in time management is failure to recognize the *amount* of time necessary to complete a task. This can work either way—either you *underestimate* and fail to recognize just how *much* time a task requires, or you *overestimate*.

Sometimes I have found it beneficial to work on a particular task for a short amount of time rather than tackling the task with no time constraints. Especially on such projects as painting, wall-papering, or sewing, it's easier for me to get wrapped up in the project to the neglect of other responsibilities; such projects could be qualified exceptions. However, by placing a limited amount of time on a task, I am able to get something done on various tasks that need attention instead of all of my attention being devoted to a singular area.

If you find yourself arriving late more times than not, allow yourself more preparation time to be ready to walk out the door. This will give allowance for the unexpected that may be contributing to the late factor.

Recognize the value of your time, and protect it. You are the steward of your own life. Just the other day, a man had come to our house to do some work. At one point, we were talking nonbusiness. I had *had* the intention of going somewhere to do something, but *I* did not speak up and say that I needed to get going; plus, *I* kept talking. This was *my* fault.

Failure to Set Goals and Plan

I have not done real well in this area. At times, I have failed to recognize the necessity of having goals, setting goals, or making plans to achieve those goals. The lack of a clear vision can mess us up (Proverbs 29:18). Having vision gives us *hope* for today and tomorrow. We have something to look forward to, something to live for, a goal to attain. Without vision, we have a tendency to plunk along aimlessly. We may be making progress, but chances are it's hindered.

If we fail to set goals and make plans to achieve those goals, all the little things can eat up our time, and we will find ourselves at the end of the day having accomplished much but little of that which we would have preferred. The little things can stand in the way of what truly matters (Song of Solomon 2:15).

Do not think that you are *too busy* to sit down and set goals and make plans. If you don't take time to do this, time will slip away one day at a time, one month at a time, and one year at a time until you find yourself at a place you didn't intend to be.

There were times when I would have lofty goals in my heart or head pertaining to a birthday or Christmas, but the goals did not always take concrete form. And although I knew in my *head* that there were certain steps that I needed to take to get to my goal, quite often, there was not much formulation of a well-thought-out plan of action. This haphazard approach applied to various areas of my life—housecleaning, paperwork, grocery shopping, and even social and family relationships.

The goal of writing this book has been one that I have had for years. Part of the reason that it has taken me so long to complete it is failure to plan and lack of diligence. These two factors flipped in the opposite direction equate to a plus in the area of life skills (Proverbs 21:5). I have prayed to God regarding diligence.

Even God Himself plans. He's the Master planner, and His plans on our behalf are great ones full of hope to ensure us bright futures! (Jeremiah 29:11). Jeremiah 29:11 is one of my favorite verses in the Bible. It would be good for us to follow His example of thinking and planning ahead. Aim high!

Tap into God, and pursue the God-appointed destiny for which you were created. Develop your passions to further His kingdom, and you will be enriched. You will come alive!

Procrastination

Perfectionist thinking (You know the thought—*Do it right*) may tell you that if you don't have the time right now to complete a task, don't even start it. Recognize that if you do even a little, it's better than doing nothing. Once started, you might find yourself completing the task in less time than originally estimated. Even if you don't finish the task, you will have the satisfaction of knowing you at least made improvement.

Another thought is to give yourself a little incentive. Upon tackling a task, even though it be brief and possibly incomplete, treat yourself to something you enjoy; I don't necessarily mean something to eat or drink. It could be a short walk, a phone conversation with a friend, or time on a creative activity.

Alternating activities is also helpful. You can alternate the challenging task with other tasks, continually returning to the challenging task, thus accomplishing that which seems daunting, little by little.

Easily Sidetracked

It is *very* easy for me to get sidetracked! I have to sometimes consciously stay focused. Within my home, while attempting to accomplish a task, I can get tempted to add an *unrelated* task to the equation because of something that gets my attention before I complete the original task. A little of this may be okay, but at times, I have to watch what I'm doing. Add this sidetracking component to someone who does not do well at planning, and it doesn't work too well.

Sidetracked + Failure to Plan = the Haphazard Approach

I'm the type of person who has trouble talking and doing something at the same time. I can *walk* and visit with someone, but if I do dishes and visit with someone, one or the other task is going to suffer. Without cruise control, I am one of those drivers whose accelerator pedal goes up and down in accordance with my mouth.

My idea of multitasking is having the washing machine and dryer doing something while *I* am doing something else; generally, it is not *me* doing two things at once other than maybe listening to the TV, Internet, radio, and so on while I'm doing work that does not require much head effort (e.g., washing dishes, baking, sewing, laundry).

I cannot have too much intellectually stimulating audio going on in the background while I am doing paperwork, though. Fluff in the background is okay. If it's intellectual or biblical teaching that I might be interested in, it is too distracting while I'm trying to concentrate on paperwork.

Another aspect of being easily sidetracked is to consider your time. Give thought to the time element involved regarding whatever it is that may be drawing you away from your original plan.

Obsessing on Religion/God

I've heard it said that people with OCD can obsess over religion or God or something like this. I have not delved into this in formal counseling. I will acknowledge that I have spent a lot of time praying, reading the Bible, and going to Bible studies, church, and church-related functions. I also am definitely not the same person I used to be. My Father has hidden me in Him. Every year, I am changing. Jesus *is* my life (Colossians 3:3–4).

I have also believed that I have had a calling of God upon my life. To be an author and public speaker incorporating Scripture would be to me the best job in the whole world. That is where the desire of my heart is. In light of this, to a degree, I think it natural that I would gravitate to Scripture, biblical teaching, prayer, and so on.

Also, the revelation of clearer understanding of God's plan of salvation was a pivotal point of change leading to healing for me in the realm of OCD. Praise God! Having recognized that truth from God and His Word has procured freedom for me, it is no wonder that I would continue to delve into His Word, looking for more and more truth.

However, I *do* acknowledge that there have been times of lengthy prayer or reading of God's Word while other responsibilities awaited my attention. Some of the issues mentioned in this book may have been factors in this regard—among which are lack of planning, time management issues, and a skewed sense of balance.

Other times, I have behaved thusly, coping with personal issues. At times, I suspect I didn't recognize the need to trust God and allow Him time to answer my prayers. I *do* acknowledge that I may not have always chosen the best ways of dealing with life issues. These extraordinarily long periods of prayer and Bible reading are becoming less frequent as I have been making life changes, becoming more aware of unhealthy thinking and behavior, being proactive regarding the well-being of my soul, recognizing some of the pitfalls mentioned in this book, and becoming healthier and happier.

Compulsive Behavior

I have lived out many compulsive-behavioral moments in my lifetime. For many of these experiences, I did not *know* that they fell into the category of compulsive behavior; there was a time when I wasn't even *aware* of the term *compulsive behavior.*

There is one biblical example that readily comes to mind that I believe portrays compulsive behavior—that is the story of Saul in 1 Samuel 10:8 and 13:8–14. In 1 Samuel 10:8, the prophet Samuel had given instructions to Saul. Saul was to go ahead of the man of God to a specified location. The prophet would come later. There would be offerings unto God. Saul was to wait a defined period of time until Samuel would come, at which time further directions would be given to him.

Saul waited the specified number of days in accordance with Samuel's directions, but where was Samuel? On top of that, Saul was concerned about what was going on with those around him. Saul made the decision to make an offering. After the offering was finished, the prophet showed up.

Samuel wanted to know what happened. Saul had his reasons—he had observed people leaving, Samuel didn't show up in the expected time frame, and on top of that, Saul was conscious of the movement of the enemy. Saul was fearful of what the enemy might do, and he desired God's favor. Thus he forced himself to do the offering.

The prophet Samuel let Saul know that he hadn't chosen wisely. He hadn't followed God's directions. Had Saul chosen differently, it would have resulted in a good future for his kingdom. As a consequence of Saul's choice, his kingdom would be removed from his hands and given to another. Saul's successor would be more in tune with the heartbeat of God, and this is the kind of man who would govern God's people, because Saul did not walk in obedience to what God had commanded.

Anyone who has dealt personally with obsessive-compulsive disorder understands the concept of forcing oneself to do something. It's like you force yourself to do or say something even though you have this uneasy feeling about doing or saying it. We allow the *compulsion* to do the unnecessary to fix what is troubling us; we allow the compulsion to override God's wisdom. Our thinking pattern is faulty. For our own well-being, we need to realize that God has so much better and healthier ways of coping and dealing with life's circumstances and the positions it presents.

Also notice the consequence of Saul's actions. There are consequences for our choices. All who have lived out compulsive-behavioral tendencies have also experienced the backlash or negative consequences of such unhealthy behavior. But thanks to God, we may "therefore come boldly unto the throne of grace, that we may obtain mercy, and find grace to help in time of need" (Hebrews 4:16 KJV).

In the definition of the Greek word for *grace*, *charis*, it states, "A favor done without expectation of return; absolute freeness of the lovingkindness of God to men finding its only motive in the bounty and freeheartedness of the Giver; unearned and unmerited favor …"[7] His *mercy* lessens the severity of the consequences that we would have normally suffered. Together, these beautiful gifts of God's grace and mercy help us to get through whatever messes we may have gotten ourselves into.

Give everything in your life to the Lordship of God. The more that you resist responding out of compulsion, the less frequent will be the compulsive behavior in your life (James 4:7).

CHAPTER 8

Constructive Ways of Overcoming OCD

Subtitles

Pray in Jesus's Name
Pray Scripture Back to God
Speak Life, Not Death
"Be Transformed by the Renewing of Your Mind"[8]
Immerse Yourself in the Word of God
Plead the Blood of Jesus
Know Who the Enemy Is
Be Aware of the Enemy's Devices
Recognize the Spiritual Realm
See Beyond the Natural and into the Spiritual Realm through Eyes of Faith
See Yourself the Way God Sees You
Bring "Every Thought Captive to the Obedience of Christ"[9]
Adopt an Overcoming Attitude
Realize that God Will Supply Everything You Need
"Live by the Spirit"[10]
Listen for that "Still Small Voice"[11] of God

Medication and Counseling
Be Prudent
Conquering Clutter
Conquering Paper Clutter

Pray in Jesus's Name

One of the best ways to deal with obsessive-compulsive disorder is to pray. God has blessed us with the awesome privilege of prayer.

> The effectual fervent prayer of a righteous
> man availeth much.
> —James 5:16 (KJV)

This verse refers to the "prayer of a *righteous* man." We are not righteous in God's sight because we do good or because of our *own* righteousness; we are *righteous* through our position in Jesus Christ. For our benefit, Jesus, who was sinless, became our sin, and through our relationship with Him, we became His righteousness (2 Corinthians 5:21). Stepping aside from dos and don'ts, God's righteousness has been made known, with credence given by two reliable witnesses, His Law and His Prophets. This is a righteousness attained through a relationship with Jesus (Romans 3:21–22).

Imagine the privilege of having a personal audience with the president of the United States. We would feel honored and excited and would tell our family and friends all about it. At the appointed time, we would be escorted in and have limited time to spend with the president. However great an opportunity an appointment with the president of the United States would be, it pales in comparison to a personal audience with the Creator of the universe and all of mankind, God Himself. We are not limited to a specific appointment time to talk to God. We can come to Him anytime, night or day, all day and all night if we so choose. Isn't that great?

When you pray, pray in the name of "Jesus." In John 14:13, Jesus encouraged His disciples to pray in His name, promising that He would do whatever they requested in His name. In the process, this would bring glory to God, His Father.

Salvation is found in no other than Jesus; in Him alone does our salvation rest. It is one name only, that being *Jesus*, that embodies our salvation (Acts 4:12). God's word and His name are magnified (Psalm 138:2).

An example of praying in Jesus's name would be to conclude your prayer(s) with "in Jesus's name I pray. Amen." There is power in the name *Jesus*.

There are many *false* gods out there that people pray to, but John 17:3 references that there truly is only one God (also 1 Corinthians 8:4). If you're going to take the time and make the effort to pray, you want to make certain that your prayers are being heard, so make sure that you are praying to the one trustworthy God. Jesus is inseparable from His Father (John 10:30). Realize for yourself today, and let it be rock solid in your heart that He alone who is to be worshiped as God is the LORD (Deuteronomy 4:39).

Pray Scripture Back to God

Don't pray words that are primarily a litany of what's wrong. Incorporate the Word of God into your prayers. As you *pray* God's Word back to Him, I believe that you are putting more substance to your prayers and giving God more to work with. It's like you're bringing out the big guns.

For example, let's say that you are talking to God and saying such things as "God, I am having such a lousy day. I overslept. Sam didn't want to get out of bed and get ready for school. I got tied up in traffic on the way to work, and now I just found out that I might be needed to work over tonight. Please help me!"

Compare that with saying all of the above but adding, "God, help me to keep my mind 'stayed on Thee,' because Your Word says that, 'Thou wilt keep *him* in perfect peace, *whose* mind *is* stayed *on thee:* because he trusteth in thee' (Isaiah 26:3 KJV).

"And Your Word also says, 'God *is* our refuge and strength, a very present help in trouble' (Psalm 46:1 KJV).

"So, Father, please help me so that the rest of my day goes smoothly. Thank You. In Jesus's name I pray. Amen."

Effective words that pour forth from the lips of one in right standing with God do a lot of good! (James 5:16).

One way to ensure victorious living is to find a specific promise within the Word of God and pray that promise back to the One who made that promise, the One who is always faithful! Among the most valuable gifts God has given us are His beautiful and tremendous promises by which we participate with God's supernatural nature (2 Peter 1:4). Even if *we* don't keep our word, *God* is always faithful to His word; He does not break a promise (2 Timothy 2:13).

Speak Life, Not Death

The words of God are powerful! The book of Genesis tells of His creative words at work in creation. God spoke, and things that we perceive with our natural senses came into being—light; space between that which is above and below; the gathering of waters and the appearance of land; vegetation with seed for future generations; the sun and the moon and the stars to be signs to man of seasons and time, day and night; and all of the animals and critters that have walked the earth (Genesis 1:3, 6–7, 9, 11, 14–15, 24).

Originally, mankind was created in God's image (Genesis 1:27).

Thus, we, too, have creative power in the words that we speak. We have the power to speak *life* to others and circumstances, and we have the power to speak *death*. We are producing fruit, either good or bad, from the words that come forth from our tongue (Proverbs 18:21). We can speak sickness or health, doom and gloom, or hope and optimism and words that edify or words that tear down.

For those who follow Jesus, we can *speak* and *pray* the Word of God over our lives and our family, friends, or anybody, and when God Almighty hears one of His own praying His very words, He is watchful to make sure that what He promised happens (Jeremiah 1:12). God's angels, who are mighty, cooperate with Him, obeying His voice in this creative work (Psalm 103:20).

Do not speak of OCD as *belonging to you*. For example, do not say, "*My* OCD …" Also do not say such expressions as "*my* cancer, *my* arthritis, *my* depression, *my* anxiety," and so on. You may be *dealing with* such things, but you do not want them to remain.

Be careful not to say such things as the following:

- I'll always be this way.
- I'll never get any better.
- My mother was like this. My father was like this, and now I'm like this; this must be my lot in life.
- I'm going to be like this the rest of my life. It is a lifelong condition.
- I must be crazy.
- I can't help it; it's just the way I am.
- I'm such a mess-up.

Instead, say things such as the following:

- I "have the mind of Christ" (1 Corinthians 2:16 KJV).
- "I can do all things through Him who strengthens me" (Philippians 4:13).
- I am better and healthier with each passing day.

- I have "a sound mind" (2 Timothy 1:7 KJV).
- I bring "every thought captive to the obedience of Christ ..." (2 Corinthians 10:5).
- God is "making all things new" in my life (Revelation 21:5).
- I am "the head and not the tail." I am above and not beneath (Deuteronomy 28:13).
- I refuse to live life afraid (2 Timothy 1:7).

Just as God spoke and His words came to pass, we, too, have the power to speak life-filled words and see those words come to fulfillment in our lives. Sometimes, I like to preface such positive professions by saying, "In the name of Jesus ..." As you continue in and become more acquainted with the Word of God, the Holy Spirit will draw attention to more verses that would be good for you to speak out of your mouth for your life and circumstances.

These positive professions do not have to be limited to exact quotations of Scripture, but they *do* need to be biblically based, for example,

In the name of Jesus,

- I live a happy life.
- My life is filled with much sunshine, in the natural and metaphorical sense.
- I am an excellent housekeeper.
- I keep my car clean.
- Our house and yard are not cluttered with stuff.
- I tend promptly to my responsibilities.
- I have a good sense of humor.
- I live up to my potential.
- We have a great marriage.
- Our family ties are strong and vibrant.

You get the idea. The list is endless. We have more power over our lives and destiny than what some of us have known or imagined. Faith is a valuable commodity. It will be manifested through the words that we speak. Positive results will follow. Don't allow what *seems* impossible to your intellect to prevent you from believing and speaking bold, life-filled professions into your life (Matthew 17:20).

"Be Transformed by the Renewing of Your Mind"[12]

It is only natural for those who have not been born again to live in the natural and see and think as the world sees, thinks, and lives. But for those who have been born again by God's Spirit, our thinking needs to come up higher. We are now His children, and our thinking needs to line up with *His* thinking.

Unless we allow the Holy Spirit access to our thought life, our thoughts do not compare to the magnitude of God's thoughts. Our ways would fall far below God's best for us (Isaiah 55:8–9).

To overcome obsessive-compulsive disorder, your thinking needs to change. You want to adopt a new mind-set of dealing with life and various situations. However they got established, faulty thinking patterns took hold in your mind, and they are causing bad results in your life. The way to affect this necessary change is to change what is going on in your *mind* (Romans 12:2).

In this change process of the mind, start with Scripture, the very words of God Himself, the One who created you. When there is a defect in a product, who is there better to go to than the designer or manufacturer? Read, listen to, meditate on, memorize, pray, study, and speak Scripture.

Remember the *power* of God's Word; these words are not mere, ordinary words printed upon pages of parchment. They are not comparable to the type on printed sheets of newspaper or the pages of a history book; they are the very words of God Himself! When you read a newspaper or book, the words impart knowledge or some type of message to your brain. When read with a sincere heart and prayer to God, who is living, the words of the Bible have potential not merely to impart knowledge of facts to your brain but to change your very life! They are able to effect desired change in the way that we think. His word is able to get through to us in a way that no one else has been able to. We will see clearly and have different perspectives (Hebrews 4:12).

You need truth to overcome OCD. God's "word is truth" (John 17:17). You need something that you can trust and count on, something that won't let you down. You need something that is going to work.

Immerse Yourself in the Word of God

To facilitate this desired change, immerse yourself in the Word of God. As you do so, God will reveal truth to you, truth that you need to correct faulty thinking. Jesus made a promise to His followers. As they lived, breathed, and walked in His word, they would show themselves to be His true followers. As a result of being dependent upon His words, truth would come to them. This truth would give birth to freedom (John 8:31–32).

As you *read* God's Word prayerfully, you will *hear* God speaking to you. You might not hear Him audibly, but you will sense in your spirit that God is speaking directly to you right then and there. Sometimes the experience is so real that it will bring tears to your eyes. You will know that what you are reading is meant directly for you. He will meet you where you're at. Sheep recognize the voice of their shepherd. He knows them intimately and gives them clear direction (John 10:3).

By *hearing* God's spoken words, you will be increasing your faith. Take the opportunity to listen to anointed preaching and teaching of God's word whether in church, at a home Bible study, or from a media source (Romans 10:17).

Feed upon the Word of God. When God supernaturally

fed the Israelites manna while they were in the desert, He was showing them and us our dependency upon not only physical food but heavenly food—all the words that come from His mouth (Deuteronomy 8:3).

God wants us to be constantly mindful of His Word. I cannot stress enough the importance of God's Word in our lives! *Live* in the Word of God on a day-to-day basis, not just on Sunday mornings or Christmas and Easter. Don't attempt to confine God to a box in your life. He *is* your life, your very life. The writer John's greatest joy was knowing that his followers were living in accordance with the truths that God gives His children (3 John 1:4).

Keep in mind the proper application of Scripture. You may be reciting Philippians 4:13, "I can do all things through Him who strengthens me," as you are cleaning house. That is well and good. However, it may *not* be God's will for you to apply this verse as you are working yourself ragged to three o'clock in the morning! This is why it is good to continue to study the Bible in order that we may know correct interpretation and application, having the author's approval as we represent Him here on earth (2 Timothy 2:15).

As you abide and walk in the Word of God, as you feed upon, read, study, hear, speak, and pray the Word of God, you will grow in your relationship with the Lord, and He will divulge truth that you need to be set free (Acts 17:28).

Plead the Blood of Jesus

When God was about to deliver His people the Israelites from bondage to slavery at the hands of the Egyptians, the blood of a lamb, applied in a specific manner given by God, was a sign to spare them from judgment against the Egyptian false gods. This judgment would affect the homes of the Egyptians but not the homes of God's people (Exodus 12:7, 12–13).

The fatal result was the death of the Egyptian firstborn, encompassing the hierarchy down to the lowliest, from throne to dungeon. This even reached the Egyptian cattle, but God's chosen people were spared (Exodus 12:29–30).

The blood of the lambs that died on behalf of the Israelites is symbolic of the one and only spotless Lamb of God, Jesus, who died on behalf of all sinners. Just as the blood of an animal was a sign of protection for God's chosen people, the blood of Jesus, the spotless Lamb of God, is *our* protection.

However, even though Jesus *did* suffer and die on behalf of *all* mankind, our salvation is not automatic. We must *accept* the gift of salvation for ourselves by faith. The following verses are among my absolute favorite!

"For by grace you have been saved through faith; and that not of yourselves, *it is* the gift of God; not as a result of works, that no one should boast" (Ephesians 2:8–9).

Just as the Israelites were instructed to apply the blood of the lamb in a specific manner to their homes to ensure their salvation, apply the blood of Jesus to yourself by asking Jesus to be your Savior, to save you from your sins.

Just as when a defendant is in a courtroom before the judge and enters a plea, you, too, can plead the blood of Jesus over yourself. An example of what you can say is, "I plead the blood of Jesus over me, spirit, soul, and body. I plead the blood of Jesus over my past, present, and future. I plead the blood of Jesus over every good plan that God has for my life. I plead the blood of Jesus over my thought life. I plead the blood of Jesus over all that I possess. I plead the blood of Jesus over my spouse, my marriage, my family, and my home." You can pray for as short or long a time as the Spirit may lead you.

The book of Revelation tells us that through the most precious blood of Jesus and the life-maintaining words that come forth from our mouths, we overcome! (Revelation 12:11). The blood of Jesus gives us protection from our enemy the devil, which leads me to the next point—know who your enemy is.

Know Who the Enemy Is

Whether we have chosen to follow Jesus, we each have a foe, and he is the devil (also called Lucifer and Satan). He has thought-out, deliberate schemes to bring about our demise, whether we be young or old, male or female. Even though it may *seem* at times that it is a tangible *person* in our lives whom we deem to be our enemy, the real enemy at work is Satan and his hierarchy of wicked spiritual cohorts in the underworld of darkness (Ephesians 6:11–12). We need to be aware and watchful, because our enemy is like a ravenous, ferocious beast after his prey—us (1 Peter 5:8).

The devil is *not* your friend, and hell is *not* one wild party! Hell is horrible torment, and hell is real. The devil is out to torment you in this lifetime as well as in the life hereafter. The devil desires the worst for us; God desires and gave His best for us. Satan is in opposition to God, His people, and all good that God represents.

The devil is a thief, and his mode of operation is stealth, death, and destruction of anybody and anything that represents good in our lives by any way that he is able to pull it off. His highest enemy, our Creator, is just the opposite. He champions our best, and whatever He does, it is with that goal in mind (John 10:10). The main objective for Jesus's coming to earth in the first place was to be our Superhero against our foe and demolish all of Satan's evil works (1 John 3:8).

Do not be deceived. Satan is the master of deception; he is crafty. He may come in an *obvious* form of darkness, especially if that is what one chooses to embrace, but often, he comes in *subtlety*, making that which is evil appear good. He will present something evil as being good while hiding the negative consequences of choosing his course (Genesis 3:1; Revelation 12:9). Jesus described Satan as a liar and a murderer. Lying originated with him, for that is his nature; he and truth are polar opposites (John 8:44).

Do not fall for the deception that there is no devil; Satan would love that. How much easier it would be for him to wreak havoc in our lives if we do not even realize he exists. Failure to acknowledge his existence is failure to acknowledge the enemy. Failure to acknowledge the enemy is failure to know how to effectively win the battle in which we find ourselves. No matter our reasoning for the way we believe, *not* believing truth does *not* make it so; truth remains truth whether it is believed or not.

Although Satan is an evil reality, he is a defeated foe. Although he is doing whatever evil he can in our lives while we walk this earth, his time is limited (Revelation 12:12).

Until Satan's demise is complete, he continues to destroy the lives of men, but our protection is in the blood of Jesus. Jesus triumphed over the devil through His suffering, the shedding of His most precious blood, His death on a cross, and His resurrection from the dead nearly two thousand years ago. The most lethal attack of the devil did not stand a chance against the most powerful Force in the universe, the essence of life itself. Jesus lives to die no more. He has taken His seat in heaven to the right of His Father. He has triumphed over death, not only for Himself but also on our behalf (Revelation 1:17–18; Colossians 3:1).

Be Aware of the Enemy's Devices

In tactical warfare, it is wise to be aware of the enemy's plan of attack. Likewise, in the midst of our spiritual warfare, we need to be aware of Satan's schemes (2 Corinthians 2:11).

Satan is crafty and deceptive; he is a liar and a murderer. Among his big guns are stealth, death, and destruction (John 10:10). God will not force Himself upon you; Satan pushes and forces. He only wants his way; he does not care about us. The Spirit of God lovingly corrects to save us from poor or unhealthy choices; Satan *accuses* to crush us like a bug (Revelation 12:10).

In your resistance to obsessive-compulsive tendencies, if you find yourself messing up, don't fall for the devil's tactic of accusation. God comes to build up; the devil comes to tear down. In fact, Satan will not only tempt you to do wrong, but then after you have succumbed to his will, he will beat you up for it. Don't allow yourself to be negatively affected by words that would beat you down, whether the words are in your own head or come from the mouths of others. You can glean from the comments of others, but if such comments were addressed in a harsh, condescending tone, don't allow the *delivery* to influence you in a bad way. Recognize that just as people who struggle with OCD do not completely understand why they do what they do, someone who has *not* had that experience would understand it even less. Others probably get frustrated in the midst of genuine concern.

The devil deals in extremes; God is balanced. Satan tries to get us to veer off of the path that God has mapped out for each one of us. Satan probably doesn't care which way you veer off as long as you turn off the path God has for you; stay focused on your unique God-ordained path (Proverbs 4:27). You can be extremely loose or rigid. Recognize that there is such a thing as trying too hard (Ecclesiastes 7:16).

In the following chapter, there are more examples of ways that Satan would try to torment us. These examples are accompanied by more detailed explanations and advice.

Recognize the Spiritual Realm

There is a heaven, and there is a hell. There is a God, one God, and there is a devil. There are angels, and there are demonic spirits. There is the natural, and there is the supernatural; there is the seen, and there is the unseen. There *is* a spiritual realm and activity, both good and evil, that is taking place that we may or may not see. Recognition of these facts will help you be better equipped to overcome OCD.

There is a story in the Old Testament in 2 Kings 6:15–17 that gives us an example of the existence of the spiritual realm that was not initially *visible* to the human eye. A prophet prayed, and Elisha's servant was able to see into the spiritual realm.

Realize that sometimes when you might be dealing with goofy thoughts associated with OCD, you could be experiencing an attack from Satan's camp. Although we *do* have a very real enemy of our soul, God does not leave us defenseless. He commissions His angels in this fight of good versus evil.

Angels are spiritual beings who have been commissioned by their Creator to minister to and help any- and everybody who will ultimately know God personally (Hebrews 1:14). One of their duties is to guard and protect created man who would one day be God's own (Psalm 91:11–12).

Angels are very powerful, godly warriors (Revelation 12:7–9). Angels are real, and they are not merely pretty beings who float in the air, beings people think fondly of, fashion figurines after, put beautiful artistic renderings of on pictures, and so on. They are very numerous, strong, and mighty and were created by God for purpose (Revelation 5:11).

Do not allow yourself to be fearful or intimidated by the revelation of Satan and his cohorts and his attacks against you. Focus on God, who He is, and His immense love for you (John 14:1; 1 John 3:1).

Jesus became like man that He created. Through His death by crucifixion, He took all of the wind out of Satan's sails. Death was Satan's maximum weapon of destruction, but it had no hold on Jesus. Because of Jesus's triumphant resurrection, we can live free from the torment of death (Hebrews 2:14–15).

Satan is a defeated foe. After detonating and demolishing the enemy's arsenal, Jesus publicly showed Himself victor (Colossians 2:15). In this great battle between good and evil that is transpiring before our eyes, God has revealed in His Word that *He* is the victor, so choose to be on the winning side.

See Beyond the Natural and into the Spiritual Realm through Eyes of Faith

Not only is it imperative that we *recognize* that there is a spiritual realm, but we also need to be able to *see* beyond the natural, that which is seen with the naked eye and perceived with the five senses, and into the spiritual realm. Now I am *not* saying that we must be able to see angels, the devil, and evil spirits—although that sometimes happens. The narrative of Elisha and his servant in the previous section is an example of being able to see into the spiritual realm.

What I *am* saying is that we need to learn to see through the eyes of faith, faith in God and in His Word, and not view present circumstances with our natural senses only. God's Word trumps circumstances every time. So often the outward negative circumstances manifested to our natural senses are a delusion. I am not denying the reality of negative circumstances, but there is so much more to our situation than what the natural senses are able to comprehend. The devil loves to cause our attention to be *problem*-focused. He wants us to lose hope, think that we'll never get out of this one, believe that we're all washed up, and call it quits. Satan likes to get us thinking that our problems are worse than what they really are. God wants our attention to be on *Him*, *His* goodness, *His* power, and *His* unending love for us.

Faith in God is one of our tools for living a great life (1 John 5:4). It involves believing in that which is not yet manifest to the natural senses (Hebrews 11:1). God desires us to learn to walk another way—one of faith, not relying *merely* upon our physical senses and the mind's comprehension (2 Corinthians 5:7).

Just as there is *negative* activity taking place in the spiritual realm, there is *positive* activity also taking place unperceived by the natural senses. An analogy in the natural world would be that of a patient who is ill with an infection on his hospital bed. He has a fever; his face is flushed. He is sick to his stomach and just doesn't feel well. Meanwhile, inside his body, an antibiotic is starting to fight the infection. The manifestation of the antibiotic's work has not yet been made evident to the natural eye.

Likewise, circumstances in our lives can appear very messed up to our natural senses, but as we place our hope in a loving Father God, persevere, pray God's promises, read and confess the Word, and are obedient to His leading, our lives, too, will begin to manifest the reality of the truth of God's Word for our lives. The outward mess will begin to fall away, and the unseen beauty and order of God will prevail (2 Corinthians 10:7). Focus your vision away from the tangible, and learn to see that which you've never seen before; the tangible is temporary, but invisible things are forever (2 Corinthians 4:18).

See Yourself the Way God Sees You

In the natural, it may not look as if you're on top. In fact, you may have experienced rejection, low self-esteem, loneliness, frustration, depression, and confusion and may feel like you just don't fit in. Just because others may have rejected you does not mean that *God* has rejected you; it could be just the opposite. Just because you feel that you're not of much good does not make it so. Be encouraged.

Those called by God have not always been wise the way the world sees wise; nor are they always among the strong and powerful or prominent in society. Qualities that some view as base, weak, and foolish are elevated in God's economy to nullify that which was erroneously viewed as wise and strong. The very ones who have been looked down upon according to the world's standards are the ones to be handpicked by God, and the world's wisdom is met with shame. Man was created to be dependent upon his Creator! (1 Corinthians 1:26–29).

Be careful specifically of how you view yourself in your *own* mind. Do not allow OCD to define who you are in your own mind; OCD is not who you are! We need to see ourselves through

God's eyes, through the eyes of faith. We can do that by heeding what *He* says about us in His Word.

There is a good example of this principle in the Old Testament in the book of Judges 6:11–16. While Gideon was saving the wheat from the hands of the Midianite enemy, he had an angelic encounter and was greeted with a salutation of noble words. Gideon was focused on all the calamity that had befallen his people and was perplexed by the contrast of comparison with the mighty deeds of God that he had heard about in the lives of his ancestors. Nevertheless, Gideon was being confronted with God's call upon his life to deliver God's people. Gideon didn't know how this could happen; he was viewing his family and himself from a natural perspective. The LORD assured him of His presence and the ensuing victory over Midian.

Gideon was viewing things and himself as they appeared in the natural realm. Here he was, trying to protect the crop from enemy hands, and God was calling him a valiant warrior! Gideon wasn't seeing himself that way. God sees our potential; He knows what we are capable of. Many times, we sell ourselves short. We allow the negative comments or reactions of others to determine our self-perception.

Be careful how you see yourself. If you are down on yourself, discouraged, and lack hope for your future, see yourself through God's lens of infinite, intimate, passionate, and tender love for you. We can be thankful to our beautiful Creator, because when He made us, it was a wonderful thing! Everything He does is wonderful. It is a beautiful thing to know this deep within our souls (Psalm 139:14).

Bring "Every Thought Captive to the Obedience of Christ"[13]

You may have even received a medical diagnosis of obsessive-compulsive disorder, but that does not mean that you are doomed to a life-as-always as you presently know it or a life shackled by OCD! Jesus came to bring healing to wounds that no one else can see, to set the captives free, and to speak a newfound freedom to those who have been imprisoned whether it be of spirit, soul, or body (Isaiah 61:1).

Life involves change. You didn't start your life out living with OCD; you don't have to finish your life with OCD! If somewhere along life's journey, you acquired an OCD mind-set, it is possible to change again and forsake it! *Impossibility* is not in the equation (Luke 1:37). Our lives begin anew with each passing day (Revelation 21:5).

Don't dwell on the mistakes of your past. God is not stuck in our yesterdays or even today. Through Him, we can live new lives now. Father God, please awaken our spiritual senses to recognize what You are doing and what You desire for us. In the aridness of our life challenges, God will provide a roadway. Our thirst for wholeness and great living will be quenched by abundant waters that only He can give (Isaiah 43:18–19).

If you know Jesus personally, you are not the same person as you were in your past. It is not possible to know Christ without being changed for the better. Just as we part with old clothes and buy new ones as years go by, He gives us new clothing, a new identity, and new mind-sets (2 Corinthians 5:17).

We can hope, knowing that God has a fresh supply of His goodness for us each day. When we open our eyes, He already has His lovingkindnesses in store, ready and waiting for us (Lamentations 3:21–23).

Notice a common thread in each of the foregoing statements—they all are life-filled affirmations that at times may seem to contradict logical reasoning in the natural realm, thus illustrating the importance of taking care to ensure that our thoughts are lining up with *God's* thoughts for us and our circumstances (2 Corinthians 10:5).

No matter what the thought, no matter the origin, every

thought must be weighed against God's Word. He has the final say! Your thought life is crucial! It may seem mind-boggling to consider that God gives us the ability to govern our thought life, but He doesn't command us to do anything without also giving us the power to do it. When Jesus comes into our lives, His kingdom and power come with Him (1 Corinthians 4:20).

For God hath not given us the spirit of fear; but
of power, and of love, and of a sound mind.
—2 Timothy 1:7 (KJV)

Maybe you haven't given much attention to the thoughts that you have been thinking. Pay attention to what's going on in your head. When defeating, discouraging thoughts come your way, whether from without or within, find, confess, and hold on to the Word of God. That living Word will refute the lies in your head and help you live victoriously.

Adopt an Overcoming Attitude

It may seem like you're down for the count. The devil may be coming against you, but the very Spirit of God Himself, residing within the Christian is greater than any evil spirit or Satan himself (1 John 4:4).

The experience of living with and manifesting OCD behavior is a very hard thing, but through God, we can overcome obsessive-compulsive disorder. You weren't born this way. There was a time in your life when you didn't have OCD; your life can return to that OCD-free state!

I can do all things through Christ
which strengtheneth me.
—Philippians 4:13 (KJV)

We are in the midst of spiritual warfare, but God has already revealed to us who put our trust in Him that we win! At times, the battle may seem fierce, but stay the course. With thankful hearts, victory is ours through Jesus (1 Corinthians 15:57). No matter the circumstances that we may be facing, we are assured that we come out on top because of the awesomeness of God's love on our behalf (Romans 8:37).

We can be courageous, because before we are even aware of a challenge in our lives, Jesus has already overcome on our behalf. He is not limited by the physical and scientific dimensions of time and space of this world—He created them! (John 16:33).

Speak positive, life-birthing affirmations about yourself that line up with God's Word. Deuteronomy 28:1–13 is a good source for such affirmations. Even if—*especially* if—you or your circumstances do not seem to be the portrait of the life-affirming words which are coming from your mouth, continue to speak them anyway. There is power in your words! The truth of those words will come to fulfillment as you are obedient to God's leading. It *will* get better.

You do not know what lies in store for you around the corner. It may be the very next bend in the road, the next phone call, one more conversation, or tomorrow morning that will unveil your breakthrough, so persevere! You may be crying now, but God promises us joy is coming (Psalm 30:5).

God is your way-Maker. He will make a way where there seems to be no way. God's ways of reaching out to you and helping you are endless. Just don't give up. Hold on to hope; it is a very precious commodity. More important, recognize that God is holding you up. God can even reveal wisdom for your life and circumstances to you while you're sleeping! Do not limit God in your thinking. He is always doing something new.

God is God of all that is new and fresh. Now is our spring season when we will see His creativity sprouting forth. Father, open our spiritual eyes to see what You are doing even today. He makes a path for us where we didn't even imagine the possibility. When we are in a dry place, He provides our entire beings with all of the life-sustaining sustenance that we need and desire (Isaiah 43:19).

Realize that God Will Supply Everything You Need

God is our all sufficiency. He's everything we need Him to be. He's the open-ended *I Am*. Moses of the Old Testament was commissioned by God to go before Pharaoh on behalf of the Israelites. Anticipating explaining to his fellow Israelites what he was about to do, Moses wanted to know God's *name* so that he could be prepared to voice it in the event they asked what it was (Exodus 3:13). God replied,

> "I AM WHO I AM"; and He said, "Thus you shall say to the sons of Israel, 'I AM has sent me to you'" (Exodus 3:14).

When situations seem hopeless, God is our God of hope. When Jesus walked the earth, His friend Lazarus died, but Jesus showed that He is God of what seems to be the impossible. He revealed that God has the last word. Just as Lazarus's sister Martha looked to Jesus, we can look to Him, too. Do you need a resurrection yourself or even on behalf of someone else? Do you need an infusion of new life for your body, emotions, or relationships? Jesus is your Man (John 11:23–26). All that is good and truly meaningful in life begins and ends with Him (Revelation 21:6).

Whatever you need in your life, Jesus is He. *You* fill in the blank—"I Am ______________" (Exodus 3:13–14). The statement is open-ended. He's your light in the darkness (John 8:12). He's your joy (Romans 14:17), your peace (Isaiah 9:6), your salvation

(John 3:16), your deliverance, your strength, your refuge, your rock (Psalm 18), your rest (Matthew 11:28), your health (Isaiah 53:5), and your prosperity (3 John 2).

Through your personal relationship with Jesus, you have everything you need to live a great life. Your heavenly Father is the *best* Daddy there is! He left nothing out; He covered all the bases when it comes to our provision (2 Peter 1:3).

Whatever you need, just ask your Father, your heavenly Father. He is *so* good. If it's wisdom that you need, He will not hold back. He wants you to succeed (James 1:5). Our Father delights in hearing from us and ensuring that everything is going well for us. He encourages us to ask, seek, and knock; as we do so, He promises the reception of a request, a discovery upon searching, and the opening of that which was closed. Even earthly dads don't taunt their children by giving them bad things when they ask for good things. If we ask of our Father, He would love to give us of His own Spirit (Luke 11:9–13).

Do not think that you don't have what it takes to overcome OCD. God doesn't create us and then just turn us loose to fend for ourselves. He cares about us even more than we care for ourselves! Even "the very hairs of your head are all numbered" (Matthew 10:30 KJV). He desires to help us even more than we realize. If someone doesn't want Him in his or her life, He respects that boundary and does not violate the person's free will, but He will eagerly be involved with anyone who desires and welcomes Him.

Do not think, *I can't do this*. The very God who created the universe and you, He will give you the strength that you need for all that encompasses His plans for your life (Philippians 4:13). You *can* do this. Look to God, and He will give you all that you need—strength, wisdom, discernment, understanding, prudence, comfort, help, peace, joy, a good life!

"Live by the Spirit"[14]

In order to conquer OCD, learn to walk ever in step with God's Spirit. As you do so, you won't be living by man's fleshly desires. The carnal nature of man and the nature of God are like polar opposites; they repel one another like a magnet. You desire to do good; however, if your thoughts, words, and actions are independent of God and His way, you won't get the results that you're looking for. When you've learned to be sensitive to the guidance of the Holy Spirit, you will be living out the essence of God's Word (Galatians 5:16–18). God encourages us in His Word to align our living, our everyday walk, with His Spirit, simply to be in step with Him, following His lead (Galatians 5:25). As we do so, it will be a beautiful dance.

How does one do this? What does this walk look like? It means to live by the promptings, leading, and inner witness of God's Spirit with your spirit. It means to live less from your *head* and more from your *heart.* It means to be less dependent upon something having to seem logical to your mental thinking. It definitely means to be freer of the need for man's approval.

Somewhere along the way, we who have dealt with OCD got locked into thinking and operating too much from our heads and didn't learn the proper balance of operating from our hearts. I suspect one component is that, for some of us, we patterned into a way of living that is one by formula, laws, and regulations, dos and don'ts, perfectionism, and so on, subconsciously thinking that that's how life works, but it isn't, and that factored into how and why we ended up with OCD. This is *not* to say that we are unloving people, nor am I saying not to use your head, but it's like we failed to learn the resource and value that comes from paying less attention to our heads and giving more attention at times to our hearts, bringing balance to the way we live. One of my favorite Scriptures has been Proverbs 3:5–6:

> Trust in the LORD with all your heart,
> And do not lean on your own understanding.
> In all your ways acknowledge Him,
> And He will make your paths straight.

These verses are particularly good for those who are dealing with OCD, because their heads tell them to do things that go beyond the norm, such as excessive washing of their hands.

A practical application example—Let's say the thought is in your *mind* to wash your hands; yet at the same time, you're not sure whether you should or not. Most likely, this is a golden opportunity to trust God with what you don't understand, lean less on the thoughts your head may be telling you, and resist washing your hands. It's like inside of you, you are sensing *one* thing, and your head is telling you *another.* Go with your *heart* and not your *head.*

At first, it will seem like you're doing something wrong, because you have been so accustomed to operating from what your *head* is telling you. As time goes on, it will get easier. You still might feel like you're doing something wrong, but at least you will be making progress and minimizing the times that you are unnecessarily saying or doing things that hinder your enjoyment of life and your relationships with others.

And if you fail, don't get all upset about it. You *will* make progress. It has taken me a long time to make the progress that I have. At times, I still miss it, but I'm a whole lot better than I used to be, and I plan to continue to experience even more freedom.

We need to follow Jesus's example. Learn to be sensitive to the leadings and the promptings of His Holy Spirit, and save yourself a ton of grief.

Listen for that "Still Small Voice"[15] of God

Listening for God's voice is part of being guided by the Spirit, because He is truly leading and guiding His own. I remember a long time ago I didn't think I was hearing God's voice; I was most likely hearing His voice more than I realized. Those who are His *hear* Him, and He knows us, and we follow Him (John 10:27). Even though we may not be *hearing* the voice of God the same way that we hear *people* speak to us, if we are born of God, we *are* hearing His voice because God says so in His Word.

God speaks to us in many ways—through His Word, written and spoken; through His prophets (Amos 3:7; Jeremiah 35:15); through others; through experience; and through dreams (Joel 2:28). His ways of speaking to us are endless. He even spoke to Balaam through a donkey! (Numbers 22:28–33).

At this point, I would like to give special emphasis to listening for the "still small voice" of God.

> And he said, Go forth, and stand upon the mount before the LORD. And, behold, the LORD passed by, and a great and strong wind rent the mountains, and brake in pieces the rocks before the LORD; *but* the LORD *was* not in the wind: and after the wind an earthquake; *but* the LORD *was* not in the earthquake: And after the earthquake a fire; *but* the LORD *was* not in the fire: and after the fire a still small voice. And it was *so*, when Elijah heard *it*, that he wrapped his face in his mantle, and went out, and stood in the entering in of the cave. And, behold, *there came* a voice unto him, and said, What doest thou here, Elijah? (1 Kings 19:11–13 KJV)

It is possible to be raised in mainline Christianity and not be taught or realize that it *is* possible to hear the voice of God speaking to each of us directly. As time has gone on, I am learning to hear His voice.

Sometimes, we don't even *pause* to listen for God's voice, leading, or direction. Sometimes, we don't even *think* to pause to listen for His voice. We can develop new habits. If we can at least develop a mind-set of being aware of pausing to listen for His voice, we have made a start.

Secondly, we need to do it—pause long enough to listen for His loving voice. Like a little child learning to walk or any other new behavior, we probably won't always get it right in the beginning; it might be by trial and error at times. I'm not saying this is the only way to learn His voice, but if we are truly eager to know His will and do it, God is abundant in pardon, grace, and mercy.

I'm finding that it is not good for me to be *afraid* to listen for His voice—afraid because of what He might tell me. God has my best interests at heart, and how am I going to learn what His voice sounds like if I don't listen? If I don't even listen, I will be missing out on a lot. When we pray, it's not just us talking to God; prayer is meant to be a two-way conversation. I have had a lot of one-way conversations with God—me doing all/most of the talking.

Adam and Eve heard the voice of God while in Eden (Genesis 2:16–17; 3:8–19). The Israelites had heard God's words firsthand but didn't want to hear His voice directly again; they preferred to receive His words secondhand. They wanted Moses to be the middle man (Exodus 20:19; Deuteronomy 5:23–27). Moses knew God's voice intimately.

"Thus the LORD used to speak to Moses face to face, just as a man speaks to his friend ..." (Exodus 33:11).

Wow! Isn't that awesome?

The nature and character of God stays the same; they are a constant in the ever-changing circumstances of life (Hebrews

13:8). The God of yesterday who spoke to His people in the desert is the same God of today who continues to speak to His people in our earthly journeys. He is a God of relationship; He desires to commune with us.

God will not force Himself into our lives. He announces His approach. He will respect our free will, boundaries, and choices and will ask for our permission to have intimate relationships with us.

"Behold, I stand at the door, and knock: if any man hear my voice, and open the door, I will come in to him, and will sup with him, and he with me" (Revelation 3:20 KJV).

In this day of multimedia attention, the God of the universe still desires to speak to our spirit man. Quiet yourself long enough to hear His voice; you will never regret it. Don't allow your prayer time to be a one-sided conversation; give God an opportunity to speak, and then listen.

As we train our spiritual ears to distinguish and hear the voice of our heavenly Father, we will be able to listen for His advice and words of wisdom when we are faced with an OCD moment and receive the best advice we could ever get—specific to our unique experience, because He knows it all.

Medication and Counseling

Medication and formal counseling can be helpful; I have done both. If you choose to go for counseling, I would suggest that you also choose a *Christian* counselor—and not based solely on his or her acknowledgment of being a "Christian counselor." Look for one who adheres to *your* Christian walk; discern whether the two of you are on the same page spiritually. You may not agree on everything, but there needs to be a peace within you regarding the person from whom you are seeking counsel. You don't have to agree on every single theological point, but there *must* be mutual agreement on key doctrinal issues. "Can two walk together, except they be agreed?" (Amos 3:3 KJV).

Wise counsel is beneficial strategy. The more godly input that you receive from others, whether they be medical professionals, clergy, family, or friends, the more likely that victory is ensured (Proverbs 24:6).

For a variety of reasons, people may sometimes have a harder time accepting the idea of taking medication for a *psychological* issue in contrast to a *physical* issue. Sad to say, sometimes there is a social stigma in this regard, but it need not be that way. On the other end of the spectrum, one needs to be careful to have a *balanced perspective* regarding this issue in connection with faith in God's healing also. God's Spirit will lead you individually as to His course of action for *your* healing.

Our Father God made provision for our healing through the suffering His precious Son, Jesus, endured on our behalf: "[T]he chastisement of our peace *was* upon him; and with his stripes we are healed" (Isaiah 53:5 KJV).

Although I have taken medication and gone for formal counseling, the thing that helped me the most was my relationship with God and everything that flows out of that relationship. *He*, by His Spirit, is the one who spoke to me through three dreams (chapter 2). In accordance with the third dream, I became aware of imperfections in my life and have cooperated with, and hope to continue cooperating with, the Holy Spirit in removing those imperfections from my life. By knowing God personally, I have had the best Counselor in the universe! I also have a direct hotline to Him; I can call upon Him any time, night or day. In days gone by, if I was dealing with a problem, I could talk to Him about it. As I read His Word, *I* was changed; I'm not the same person I was forty, thirty, twenty, or even ten years ago. I have prayed for truth that would set me free from anything that has me bound. I have received truth from my Father. I have allowed that truth to change faulty thinking.

Be Prudent

You may be transparent and genuinely open with your feelings and matters of the heart, trusting that others will understand and have your best interests at heart, but *others* will not always understand or value your personal information the same way you do.

OCD is hard enough to understand even for the one wrestling with it, let alone someone who doesn't deal with it on a personal level. Just as with any life issue, those who have *been there, done that* can relate better with the one who is still caught in the entrapment of OCD. Others may not completely understand but will still be compassionate and empathetic, and some may not have a clue or care one iota. Some people are not comfortable or acquainted with conversing on levels of emotion and matters of the mind.

When it comes to the most precious possessions of your soul—some being your innermost thoughts, don't carelessly put them out there before just any and everybody; you could be risking your valuable words being trampled upon and the possibility of the listener turning on you, and then you'd find yourself dealing with an additional problem (Matthew 7:6).

Others may not place the same value on what is very personal and meaningful to you. When it comes to deep matters of the heart, be selective in your confidants. Do not use the workplace as an arena to air all when it comes to OCD; you don't want to jeopardize your own welfare regarding your job.

Conquering Clutter

One of the best ways of conquering clutter is to head the culprit off at the pass—watch what comes *into* your house in the first place.

Be selective about the stuff that is *offered to you* that will take up residence in your domain. Be bold enough and willing to say, "No, thank you." Ask yourself necessary questions, and pay attention to your present acquisition:

- Do I really need more T-shirts?
- Have I read the books that I presently have?
- What about the craft projects that I haven't completed?
- How many tools do I really need?

Stay away from or limit going to garage sales—and I *like* a garage sale! If you *do* go to a garage sale and see something that you like, it's a good idea to know what you intend to do with the purchased item (e.g., the bargain oil painting, the vase of flowers, the box of books). Where is it going to go? Better yet, *have* a garage sale and get rid of stuff! If others go in with you on the garage sale though, be careful about buying *their* stuff. Here are some more tips:

- Keep your eyes from wandering to what is by the curb in someone's garbage.
- Don't use your front porch as a storage unit.
- Don't use your car as a mobile storage unit on wheels.
- Within your home, do not leave things out in the open for all to see mainly because of your personal need for a *visual reminder* to tend to whatever it may be—out of sight / out of mind. To eliminate this problem, a handheld technical device is a good tool of choice. You can store all kinds of notes and lists.
- Try to eliminate or be selective as to the times that you leave things out with the intent of *resuming whatever activity* later (e.g., vacuum cleaner, ironing board, and so on).
- Be careful what you choose to stash on top of the refrigerator.

- Don't hold on to things for unhealthy reasons, such as guilt.
- Recognize that your true life is not about your possessions.

Jesus cautioned against greed. Be on the lookout. Be careful. Greed comes in different disguises; some are more obvious than others. No matter how much you have, your stuff doesn't define you (Luke 12:15).

There is a deception that can accompany our abundance of stuff (Matthew 13:22). Recognize that your time, energy, and resources are required to store and maintain everything you own. Responsibility comes in with every item that comes through your door.

Such lessons hit home when you downscale from a large family home to smaller living quarters or upon transitioning from home-living to assisted-living or upon sorting through years' worth of accumulated belongings following the funeral of a loved one.

One of the most liberating experiences I have ever had was when we had a moving sale and got rid of a bunch of stuff. We were preparing to move across country. I told my children they could keep a certain number of short-sleeved tops, a certain number of long-sleeved tops, and so on. It was great. When we moved into our new home, it was like starting fresh. We weren't burdened with too much *stuff*.

Be observant; keep your eyes and ears open to the things that work for others (Philippians 3:17). Wisdom is all around us, continually speaking wherever we are in the midst of the circumstances of our everyday lives to those who will listen (Proverbs 1:20–21).

A question to ponder is if I were to die today, would I want my family to have to go through all of my stuff and papers? This leads to the next topic—*paper clutter*.

Conquering Paper Clutter

This area is still a challenge for me, but here are some suggestions.

Miscellaneous Paper

- By processing paperwork as promptly as you are able, this will ward off piles of paper, save time and energy paper shuffling, and keep your mind freer of mental clutter.
- One thing I have found to be helpful is *not* to mix all my paper items together. Don't combine the important with the unimportant. Don't just pile everything that is *paper* on your desk—coupons, flyers, photographs, bills, unopened mail, grocery lists, and so on. It is helpful if I distribute the paper to different areas.
- Keep the grocery list, coupons, and so on in the kitchen.
- Put the photographs in one area, even if it means getting to it later.
- If you *are* going to keep advertising flyers, put them on a coffee table, end table, or better yet, a magazine rack.
- Try not to mix nonpaper "stuff" with papers.

Financial

- If it's not necessary to save a "paid" bill, don't.
- Go for the automatic payment of bills from your checking account.
- Give bills and financial obligations a priority.
- Don't wait until the due date to pay a bill; pay it *ahead* of time.
- By exercising prompt bill payment, we are being proactive in regards to time management. We avoid the risk of receiving future duplicate billings, which could result in the spending of our quality time by checking to see whether a bill has been paid.

- Prompt bill payment wards off late and delinquent fees.
- If you have a reoccurring monthly payment, consider making a one-time payment to cover twelve months. This is a time-saving step when reconciling the bank statement, because there are fewer transactions to account for.
- If you have a check to cash, put it in your wallet and put a reminder in your handheld device. That way, when you're out and about, you won't have "forgotten" the check at home.

Income Tax Applicable

- When paying anything that qualifies for income taxes (e.g., charitable contributions, property taxes) pay with a check, mark the receipt *paid* along with the check number and corresponding dollar amount, and file the receipt promptly or make record of it in the current year's income tax file.
- In the check register, mark a red R to indicate that this has already been recorded for income tax purposes. This will make it easier at income tax time.
- Upon reconciling the bank statement, watch for applicable and potential tax deductions and record them (such as things that you may have paid while away from home).

Mail

- When it comes to incoming mail, minimally, open it. Even this has been a challenge for me.
- Do not falsely assume that you automatically know what an incoming piece of mail contains simply because you are accustomed to receiving similar-looking envelopes on a regular basis. This one could be the exception; it could hold a bill or a check (this does not apply to junk mail).

- Have a stapler handy to attach papers together.
- Have stamps on hand along with return-address labels. Keep them together.

Tackling Paperwork

- Set at least a minimum amount of time to work on paperwork six days a week. A minimum amount of time is better than none at all. Once you get started, you might find yourself working longer.
- If tackling paperwork gets your mind racing, take care of it during the daytime and not before going to bed at night.
- If the radio or TV are distracting, turn them off.
- Do not view all pieces of paper as being equal. Some are more important; some are less.
- The same principle applies to the *wording* on each paper. Learn to recognize the important parts, and give those priority; skim the less important, and ignore the irrelevant (to you and your circumstances). Everything on the paper is there for a reason; you just don't need to make everything on the paper your concern.

Medical Bills / Claims

- Use a three-ring binder to file medical insurance claims with corresponding paid medical bills.
- Staple the two together, and file by procedure/appointment date with current date on top.
- Use tab dividers to separate years.
- Mark the bill paid along with the check number, dollar amount, and date paid.
- Highlight the date of the procedure.
- Upon receipt of a medical bill, if you haven't yet received the explanation of benefits form from your insurance

carrier, and the breakdown of the bill looks correct, go ahead and pay it. You can match up the explanation of benefits form later. If a discrepancy arises, it can be corrected. At least you will have paid the bill.

CHAPTER 9

Our Spiritual Armor

One of the best things that we can do to help us live victoriously is to wear our spiritual armor. There is a war taking place in the spiritual realm, and we are in the midst of it. Some of us are pawns, because we are unaware of the spiritual warfare against our souls. Just as a soldier would not dream of going into combat without his or her gear, we, too, need to be properly suited up for the spiritual warfare in which we find ourselves. Ephesians 6 describes our spiritual armor. "Put on the full armor of God, that you may be able to stand firm against the schemes of the devil" (Ephesians 6:11).

> Therefore, take up the full armor of God, that you may be able to resist in the evil day, and having done everything, to stand firm. Stand firm therefore, having girded your loins with truth, and having put on the breastplate of righteousness, and having shod your feet with the preparation of the gospel of peace; in addition to all, taking up the shield of faith with which you will be able to

> extinguish all the flaming missiles of the evil *one.* And take the helmet of salvation, and the sword of the Spirit, which is the word of God. (Ephesians 6:13–17)

When you get up in the morning, you can mentally go through these verses, name each piece of armor, and vocalize that you are placing them upon your body. You are doing this by faith; you do not see in the natural what is taking place in the spiritual.

Truth

This topic was expounded upon in chapter 5. However, I emphasize that truth can be found in God's word (John 17:17), Jesus (John 14:6), and God's Spirit, who is our guide in this arena (John 16:13). In the quest for truth, the Bible, Jesus, and His Spirit are paramount. They are each trustworthy; you need not fear that any of these will lead you astray.

Breastplate of Righteousness

We do not live our lives justified by our *own* righteousness. Our justification is a gift from God to those who place their faith in Jesus. I am *so* thankful for the revelation of this truth; not knowing this truth factored into me becoming so messed up in my thinking and thus my living. None of us are good enough on our own. None of us are perfect, and even what we deem to be our good deeds, thoughts, and actions are actually filthy as far as God's righteousness is concerned (Isaiah 64:6). Justification in God's eyes comes in the form of a beautiful gift from Him to us, wrapped in the most elegant paper of grace and tied with the gorgeous bow of redemption that Jesus provided (Romans 3:24).

No matter how hard we may try, we would never be good enough because inevitably, there would remain the sin factor, and the only remedy for the sin factor is the blood of Jesus. Everyone has sin in his or her past; none who have ever walked this earth (other than Jesus) have ever retained the fullness of God's glory (Romans 3:23).

Not by our own achievements or as compensation for our own good works but through believing in Jesus as Savior, we are gifted by Him with the beautiful qualification of right standing with our Creator (Romans 3:21–22). He, who never sinned a day in His life, gave us the best trade Wall Street will ever see; He took our sins and gave us His righteousness in return (2 Corinthians 5:21).

If you are thinking poorly of yourself or find others being hard on you because you have messed up with OCD thinking and behavior, remember this piece of armor. This also applies to situations in which the devil may be accusing you, or you may be tempted to beat yourself up; don't fall into either of these traps. You may have blown it. You may have blown it over and over again, but you're not the scum of the earth. You do not stand because of your *own* righteousness but because of the righteousness of Jesus. Ask God for His help. Get back up, and keep on keeping on.

Preparation of the Gospel of Peace

Notice that this piece of armor goes on the feet. Wear this wherever you go, wherever your feet take you. God wants us to live in peace with Him, others, and ourselves. Along with His righteousness and the joy that radiates from His Spirit in the midst of any circumstance, peace for the soul is one of the three main components of God's kingdom (Romans 14:17).

With God, it is possible to have peace even in the most dire situations because the peace that is of God is not contingent upon everything being all A-okay in our world but upon who He is, our relationship with Him, and our faith in His love for us and faith in His precious promises to us found in His Word. Before Jesus was crucified, resurrected, and departed bodily from this earthly realm, He gave this kind of peace to His disciples. This same peace is available to each of us who also choose to follow Him today. This God-peace is a divine antidote to troubles and fear (John 14:27).

The *world's* way of peace is to have everything in order, everything the way it should be; however, this is not always the way it is. *God's* way is to give us peace in the midst of the storm, not just after the storm has subsided. In the dark of night, when things tend to look the bleakest, two of God's believers prayed and sang God's praises from the midst of prison, and God not only miraculously secured *their* release but also the release of all the rest of the prisoners! (Acts 16:25–26).

Peace with God

No one likes living in a home full of strife and contention. One may say, "All I want is some peace around here!" Just as family members are *related* to one another, our Creator, God, desires *relationship* with us through our faith in His Son, Jesus, and through that relationship, He desires for us to be at peace with Him and He with us. Those who have been born again are earthly temples. The very divine being of God Himself resides within these temples of clay, and He desires peace in His home (1 Corinthians 3:16).

The source of all true peace is Father God Himself, the bestower of all that is good, pure, and lovely (James 1:17; Philippians 4:8). Jesus is "The Prince of Peace."

> For unto us a child is born, unto us a son is given: and the government shall be upon his

> shoulder: and his name shall be called Wonderful, Counsellor, The mighty God, The everlasting Father, The Prince of Peace. (Isaiah 9:6 KJV)

There was a time when we were not connected with God. Many of us didn't grow up Jewish; we weren't acquainted with the Abrahamic covenant or the rest of God's covenants and didn't know all that they entailed, including the magnificent promises that accompany them. We were lost and didn't even know it. Thank God things are different now! We, who at one time didn't even have a clue, now know and experience firsthand His peace because of His blood (Ephesians 2:12–14).

For those who put their trust in Him, God gives us the most beautiful gift of justification; this means that He views us as if we never did anything wrong! Because of this beautiful gift, we, the formerly guilty, can stand before the righteous Judge of all mankind with easy peace within our souls, absent even a trace of fear. All this is possible because of the love of Jesus for us (Romans 5:1).

Peace with Others

God desires, and I dare say that most of *us* desire, for us to live peaceably with others—whether it be family, friends, neighbors, coworkers, and so on. God gives us encouragement in a biblical mandate to live in such an order (1 Thessalonians 5:13). Peace is intentional and is meant to be pursued with everybody (Hebrews 12:14). To the best that we are able, we are encouraged to maintain peace in all of our relationships (Romans 12:18).

However, be aware that because of your stand for Christ, there may be times when peace is strained or lacking in relationships and circumstances. Jesus's message was controversial; not everyone would embrace it or Him. Jesus, His life, His ministry, and His message would divide just like a knife cuts a melon in two. Son and father, daughter and mother, in-law and in-law would be against one another. Family members would have differing viewpoints and beliefs and would be enemies (Matthew 10:34–36).

Ideally, God would want us all to be of like mind. He encourages us to do the best we can to get along with people and to be on the same page with Jesus's teachings being the plumbline. When it seems hard to do, He will bless us with the perseverance to see this thing through, and He will shower encouragement along the way. He desires to hear us glorify Him in unity (Romans 15:5–6).

Just as parents are happy to see their children getting along well with each other, our heavenly Father is happy when we His children behave in like manner by being like-minded, in sync with His Spirit, headed in one direction—God-kingdom-oriented. In concrete terms, we encourage each other and love when it isn't always easy or clear-cut. We're affectionate with kind words, hugs, and simply being there. Compassion flows from our hearts to those in the midst of trials, pain, and disappointment (Philippians 2:1–2).

It's all about Him. Do your best to be at peace with other people without compromising your own values that line up with God and His Word, which leads me to the next point.

Peace with Ourselves

Sometimes, we are harder on ourselves than others are. You may have messed up and badly at that. You may even think or feel that *you* are a mess-up, but don't allow yourself to stay there, especially in your mind. No matter how many times you may find yourself "doing it wrong" or doing goofy things, ask God for help to do better. Do whatever He tells you, and get up and keep going. Don't allow yourself to be tormented by guilt and condemnation. This is not from God!

Condemnation is *not* part of the Christian's wardrobe; Jesus threw that out of our closets a long time ago. That ugly garment is outdated and unbefitting to those called by His name (Romans 8:1). Don't be harder on yourself than what God Himself is.

Be encouraged by taking this to the bank—even when we mess up, Jesus comes for us in the midst of the troubles we got ourselves into. He won't agree with us on the position of sin, but He will save us from it. If you're wrestling with the fact that you have blown it *big*-time, be encouraged. Paul (formerly Saul) referred to himself as the biggest sinner there was. Until God got his attention in a dramatic movie-scene way, the old Paul (Saul) believed he was doing a good thing by persecuting Christians (1 Timothy 1:15).

God is in the forgiving business; He is the originator of forgiveness. He's also the God of restoration. He loves to pick us up, dust us off, turn us in the right direction, and gently lead us to that which is good for us. He is a *good* God. It's awesome to realize that even when we make wrong choices, He is able to meet us in the midst of the consequences of those wrong choices and help us to move forward. Extend the same love, kindness, grace, and mercy that you are so willing to extend to others to yourself (Matthew 22:39).

As a little baby, Moses, a Hebrew, was rescued from potential death and was raised in an Egyptian household. When he grew, he saw his own countryman assaulted. In an attempt to come to the man's aid, Moses committed murder. This is the same Moses whom, years later, God would raise up to help deliver His people out of slavery in Egypt. What Moses tried to do in his *own* way years before would now be accomplished by doing it *God's* way.

The Bible has *numerous* examples of people who sinned, and yet God continued to love them and forgive them, and they are esteemed in God's eyes and in His church body. Upon handing out the accolades of faith in chapter 11 of the book of Hebrews, God chose to include Rahab, not a town's most distinguished citizen (verse 31).

King David of the Old Testament committed adultery, which

resulted in the conception of a baby, and then he tried to cover it up by requesting the woman's husband be placed in a very perilous position at the battlefront, which resulted in the man's death! Mission accomplished (2 Samuel 11:15). Yet Psalm 51 expresses the latter repentance of David's heart.

We either forget or fail to comprehend how much God our Father loves us. Sometimes, we are too *self*-conscious and *sin*-conscious, when truly our lives are *less* about us and our sins and *more* about Him and His love. Jesus took care of the sin issue and self-condemnation a long time ago. He doesn't want us to live troubled, worried, and all worked up about everything but instead wants our hearts to be light. Believe that He is awesomely good and is radically for you in all that lines up with His kingdom (John 14:1).

You can have peace even when the world around you seems to be falling apart. God's peace transcends circumstances. We can always find something to be happy about. Knowing who God is, His nature, and His hope-filled promises to us found in His Word, we can always be rejoicing in Him. Have the tenacity of that of a bulldog. God has not abandoned you. Don't allow anxiety in the door. No matter what's going on, pray, pray, pray! With a thankful heart to God, accompany those prayers with all kinds of requests. In response, His peace, which is far beyond all of our reasoning and logical comprehension, will stand sentinel over our hearts and minds. This is all possible through Jesus (Philippians 4:4–7).

Be true to who you are in Christ—be yourself. If you don't let the true "you" shine, others will not truly know *you*. Be true to Christ, His Word, and His direction for your life.

Shield of Faith

Believing in desired things that are not yet manifest before our physical senses and having confidence that these things will be evident not only to us but to others, this is faith (Hebrews 11:1).

Apart from faith, we are not able to please God. To come before Him, it is imperative that we believe in God's existence. He is an infinitely good God who rewards all who pursue Him (Hebrews 11:6).

Even though God may not have revealed Himself personally to you by appearing in a dream or vision and although you may have never heard the audible voice of God, He still reveals Himself to man. God doesn't toy with us. He made us, loves us, and cares about us deeply and intimately. He desires us to know Him. He has revealed Himself to everyone. From the time that the world was first created, through this magnificent masterpiece of canyons, mountains, oceans, and flowers, we are awed and perceive with our physical senses the unseen nature of a divinely powerful Creator (Romans 1:19–20).

God also reveals Himself in His Word and through the testimony of eyewitnesses. For decades, there have been many eyewitnesses to the reality of God's existence, the truth and power of His magnificent word, and His marvelous involvement in the lives of His creation. For the benefit of those to come after them, these eyewitnesses diligently proceeded to make record of these testimonies and teach them to others. The truth contained in these records is paramount and worth investigation (Luke 1:1–4). The accounts of Jesus written in the Bible are not elaborate fairy tales; they are based on eyewitness testimony of the Superpower of all eternity (2 Peter 1:16).

Thomas had spent personal time with Jesus; he had heard Jesus's words personally with his own two ears. They ate together, talked together, and spent time together. After the crucifixion of Jesus came His resurrection. One may think as Thomas did—*I'll believe it when I see it and when I feel it* (John 20:25). Jesus loved Thomas; He went the extra mile to convince Thomas of His resurrection. However, faith that does not need to be substantiated by external evidence to the physical senses is a higher kind of faith and will result in blessing (John 20:27–29).

Faith, to be of benefit to us, must go beyond mere *head* knowledge; it must gravitate to the *heart.* Thoughts may be in the mind, but faith is birthed from the heart (Romans 10:10). Mental acknowledgment of God's existence is good, but this is not a *saving* faith. Even the devil believes in God's existence (James 2:19). It is possible for the right words to be coming from a person's lips and the heart not be right (Matthew 15:8).

Don't merely believe in the *existence* of God; believe in *Him.* The more we read the Bible and become acquainted with the *God* of the Bible, the more we will come to know His character and will be able to place our faith in Him and in His immutable character! There are many reasons why we might have a flawed perception of God's character, but His many facets are revealed in His Word and in His Son, Jesus, by the power of His Spirit. He is good, kind, just, awesome, majestic, mighty, all-knowing, loving, patient, full of mercy, compassionate, and gentle.

The devil hates God and does not want us to know Him or love Him or live for Him. The devil will use anybody, anything, and any circumstance to fire missiles your way—your own thoughts, human philosophy, gossip, a hurtful comment spoken in the heat of the moment, well-intentioned advice from others, factual circumstances, and even false teaching within the church body (Ephesians 6:16).

Just as we need faith to believe that God exists and that He is who His Word says He is, we need faith to live successfully in the course of our everyday living. Your marriage may be teetering, your health failing. Your children may be out of control. Maybe you're battling depression and don't even want to get out of bed in the morning or have been seriously wronged by those closest to you. Maybe you're just plain overwhelmed with life. It's not just the big things either; we need faith for the little things, too—paying the light bill, making dinner, buying groceries, fixing the toilet, making that return to the store, shoveling the sidewalks, visiting the in-laws, and so on.

Life has problems, and the devil would *love* to get us all depressed, desperate, worried, and panic-stricken. He wants us to quit, give up, give in, and throw in the towel. He tries to convince us that whatever good it is that we are believing for and holding on to will never happen. He tries to tell us that we're no good and a failure, and he tries to convince us that our existence isn't doing any good. This is why we need faith.

- The devil says it (*that which is good*) will never happen; God says it will.
- The devil says that you're no good; God says that you are the righteousness of God (2 Corinthians 5:21).
- The devil beats you up; God lifts you up.
- The devil steals; God provides.
- The devil kills; God *is* life and gives life.
- The devil tempts us to sin; God forgives.
- The devil destroys; God restores.
- The devil brings fear; God gives faith (Romans 12:3).
- The devil lies; God *is* and speaks truth (John 8:44; John 14:6).
- The devil tempts us to live by our fleshly desires; God helps us to live by His Spirit.
- The devil accuses; God encourages.
- The devil condemns; God shows us a better way.
- The devil hates us! God *is* love and loves us.

This is when it is vital to *know* the Word of God so that you can *believe* or put your *faith* in that Word and discern between truth and falsehood. What you *don't know* can jeopardize you. God says that His people suffer harm because they just don't know (Hosea 4:6).

God's "word is truth" (Psalm 119:160) and will refute the lies of Satan. As you put your faith in the truth of God's Word, you are using your shield of protection. Read and study the Word of

God regularly; this will help you be equipped to drench the fiery weapons of Satan, because you will know *what* and *Whom* to put your faith in (Ephesians 6:16).

Helmet of Salvation

A helmet protects the head. Apart from the head, your body cannot live. Just as your *physical* body is not able to live apart from the head, your *spirit* man is dead unless you have experienced salvation. Salvation is imperative. This is explained in more detail in Chapter 3—"The Good News of Salvation."

Prior to salvation, although our *physical* man was alive and well, our *spirit* man was dead on account of our wrongdoing. We each have walked the way of the earthly realm in which the demonic prince influences men, women, and children to walk in ways contrary to God's best for them. All of us, saved or unsaved, know what it's like to yield to lust in whatever area we may have legitimate needs—whether it be love, hunger, acceptance, value, and so on. We gave in to our desires and whatever our minds could conceive, not realizing that there were healthier ways to get our needs met. Just like everyone else, we reaped the consequences of our own poor choices. But suddenly our Knight in shining armor showed up! He never runs out of mercy. He can't help but love us, because that is who He is. While we were still messing up, He brought life to us by connecting us to Christ. We didn't rescue ourselves; God gets all the credit. He brought us near to Him. Positionally speaking, we have been escorted by God Himself to a heavenly seat of honor with Jesus! Jesus is our covering. This magnificent love story of a kind Creator for His created will for all eternity be magnified, showcasing His unlimited grace through His Son, Jesus (Ephesians 2:1–7).

One attack of the devil is to try to get you to doubt your salvation; I went through such a period, and it is not a good place to be. I wondered whether I had prayed the right words (to be saved) and would pray again, and again, and again. One of the factors I was most likely dealing with was legalism. As time passed, this temptation let up. No matter what you may be going through, choose God. Put your defenses up against Satan; don't merely passively accept whatever he may be throwing your way. If you give him enough resistance, he'll leave (James 4:7).

Another aspect of our helmet of salvation is that the helmet protects our mind. We must pay attention to what we are *thinking*; if it doesn't line up with God, His way, His Word, and His will, dismiss it. Our thought life is an area of utmost importance in our lives (2 Corinthians 10:5).

Philippians 4:8 gives a checklist of parameters for what we would choose to dwell upon. The more that we stay within these guidelines, the healthier our minds and lives will be. The checklist includes things that are

- true
- honorable
- right
- pure
- lovely
- good
- excellent
- praise-worthy

The more that we read and study the Bible, meditate on the Word, memorize Scripture, pray the Word back to God, pray and spend time with God, attend Bible study and Sunday school class, and sit under anointed teaching and preaching, the more that our thinking will line up with God's will for our lives. Along our life's journey, we have picked up flawed thinking resulting in faulty living. When our thinking gets corrected, our living will improve.

Don't reshape your life to fit into the world's mold. The change that is needed to truly live the good life is going to happen in the *mind*. To get the positive results that we desire, this new way of thinking will line up with God's good will, which is better than any plan *we* could come up with on our own. His way is an acceptable way (Romans 12:2).

Sword of the Spirit

The next piece of spiritual armor is "the sword of the Spirit, which is the word of God" (Ephesians 6:17). This personally is one of my favorites; I *love* God's Word! The truth of God's Word will calm your fears, bring peace to your soul, comfort your heart, dispel discouragement, and bring healing of soul and body. God's Word will propel you forward into the good things that God has in store for you.

God spoke, and those words brought health and deliverance from that which had destroyed them (Psalm 107:20).

God's word will shine a bright light on the path that we walk, revealing which way to go and any snares, traps, or potholes that we wouldn't otherwise be able to see (Psalm 119:105).

God's word will dispel confusion. To sum it all up, God's word is a trustworthy constant. Not even a trace of falsehood will be found there, and His word will exist for eternity (Psalm 119:160).

In your attacks from Satan, be sure to *use* your sword. God's Word is powerful! Don't just take whatever the devil dishes out. Demolish his lies with the Word of God as Jesus did when He was confronted with the devil's temptations (Matthew 4:1–11). Follow Jesus's example by *speaking* the Word of God. Speak, "It is written …" (written in God's Word), and complete the sentence with Scripture that is applicable to the circumstance at hand.

God's words are alive and will never die. They are working on behalf of the One who spoke them and have a precision and sharpness that surpasses that of any surgical instrument. It is hard for the human mind to fathom the unseen of where the soul ends and the spirit begins, but God's word is able to pierce this dividing line. It is also able to separate marrow from the joints and goes where sometimes we ourselves have difficulty going—our motives and thought life (Hebrews 4:12).

There is great power in the words that we speak; this power can be creative or destructive. Sometimes, our very lives are at stake; we can choose to speak life, or we can choose to speak death (Proverbs 18:21). *Speak* the Word! It will be you taking your stand against the devil, letting him know that you recognize his lies for what they are and that you are rejecting him and his lies and instead are choosing God and His abundant life. Satan hates the Word.

No one can forewarn you about every possible line of attack with which Satan might come against you. There certainly are generalities—fear, strife, adultery, murder, and so on—and also specific examples given in the Bible from which we can learn. This is why it is important for us to read and *study* the playbook, so that we can be prepared for whatever the devil might bring our way. "Study to show thyself approved unto God, a workman that needeth not to be ashamed, rightly dividing the word of truth" (2 Timothy 2:15 KJV).

At just the precise moment, the Holy Spirit will cause you to remember words from the Bible that are appropriate for the specific circumstance (John 14:26). How can the Holy Spirit cause you to remember something if you've never heard or known of it before? I realize that God in His omnipotence can *reveal* to you anything He wants at anytime, anywhere; I am simply reinforcing the importance of getting the Word inside of us.

Meditate upon the Word of God. As you do so, you will be adding to your arsenal Scriptures that the Holy Spirit will be able to call upon to remind you of the way of truth and life. As you place the treasures of God's word in your heart, that very word will help you live a life that is pleasing to the One who made you (Psalm 119:11).

Also, recognize that in the previous Scripture reference of Matthew 4:1–11, Satan tempted Jesus *with* the Word of God. Satan will try to get at *you* with the Word. This is one reason why it is imperative to be knowledgeable about the Word and its correct interpretation and application so that you can discern between truth and error and apply it correctly to your life!

Display the word of God in your home. You can even *write* the word of God on your door casings. God desires us to have His words on our hearts. As earthly parents, we continually instruct our children while they are growing up, giving them guidance on all kinds of things. Similarly, God's word needs to be part of our everyday conversation wherever we are, no matter what we are doing (Deuteronomy 6:6–9).

10

CHAPTER 10

Your Future Is Bright

Maybe you got a rough start. Maybe you started out okay but got messed up along the way, or maybe you find yourself in a big mess this very moment. Nevertheless, learn from the past, live in the present, and look forward with joyful anticipation to your future. It's a bright one. Do not allow yourself to be bound to a future of doom and gloom because of your own thinking. Line your thoughts up with the Word of God—God, who created everything in the universe, ranging from the multitude of stars in the sky to a grain of sand on the ocean's beach, is a God who has a plan. And He has wonderful plans for each of us, not plans for our demise! He encourages us with hope for our future (Jeremiah 29:11).

We have such a loving God, a loving Father. He does not want us in bondage to fear of any kind; this kind of spirit does not originate with Him. He adopts us as His own, and we call Him "Daddy" (Romans 8:15).

He is the most compassionate and loving Person you will ever know. He lavishes grace on the human race. Anger doesn't come quickly to Him. When He *does* get angry, He gets over it; He doesn't hold a grudge. He has chosen that man's sins will not squelch His love for him! He does not give us full reward for our wrongdoing. Reverence for Father God attracts His infinitely high lovingkindness. Just as east and west never meet, so He has ensured that our sins do not stick to our identity. Like a tenderhearted dad, our heavenly Father is compassionate toward His own who hold Him in reverence. The One who made us knows intricately our construction; He's well aware that our physical nature originated from the dust of the earth (Psalm 103:8–14; Genesis 3:19).

Your heavenly Father loves you so much "that He gave His only begotten Son" on your behalf to save you (John 3:16). This loving Father does not leave us to fend for ourselves and leave us alone to get out of all the trouble that we get into.

Before Jesus left planet Earth, He said that He was going to make a request of His Father. Jesus promised that the best Helper there is would be given to us from Father God. This Helper would be a constant Presence of truth. Not just anybody would be able to receive this Spirit; intimacy with God is the platform for the Holy Spirit's entrance. This Spirit would live within man. Jesus did not want to leave us on our own like orphans. He promised His return in the form of His Spirit (John 14:16–18).

What an awesome invitation that has been set before us, an offer to know intimately the very God of the universe, its Creator, a friend who sticks like glue! (Proverbs 18:24). When you hear God's Spirit knocking upon the door of your heart, I implore you to open your heart and allow Him entry to heal wherever and however your heart has been bruised. It will be the beginning of a forever lavish dining experience and the best and most important decision that you will ever make (Revelation 3:20).

As you follow the Spirit's leading and promptings, you will live a good and fulfilling life, a great life! You will live *Zoe*—the Greek word for "life" as it is used in John 3:16; this is life to the fullest! Not only will He bless you with victory over OCD, but He will lead you to triumph in every area of your life! (2 Corinthians 2:14).

God Almighty Himself will give you a makeover. As you cooperate with Him, you will become the new you. Some of you will experience happiness and a lightheartedness that you have *never* known before. He is in the renovation business—*people* renovation (Revelation 21:5).

CHAPTER 11

Advice to Family and Friends

Some of us may have exhibited OCD symptoms on one occasion or another in varying degrees—double-checking the doors to make sure that they're locked, going back to the house to make sure the coffeepot was turned off, washing your hands one too many times, can't stand it when things aren't just so—you name it. If such idiosyncrasies are *minor* (tolerable, more of a nuisance for the person exhibiting the behavior and not too intrusive into the lives of people around him or her), we can live with it and even laugh about it, but there comes a time when enough is enough. That is what this book has been about.

Another's OCD behavior or thinking may be more evident to you than it is to him or her, especially if it's the tolerable behavior as described earlier. The person in these circumstances may not even realize that he or she is exhibiting OCD behavior, but someone who has been there, done that, may see it more readily. A mild manifestation of OCD behavior may never need addressing by anybody other than the individual involved and the Holy Spirit.

In the situations where someone is dealing with obsessive-compulsive disorder in a *major* fashion, most likely, the individual already knows that he or she has a problem. He or she may not fully recognize the *extent* to which something is wrong—and then maybe he or she does. This person may realize that something is drastically wrong but not know how to get out of it. He or she needs truth—truth that explains why he or she is doing what he or she is doing. When a person says or does something, good or bad, there is a reason behind that behavior; people behave the way that they do for a reason. Pray to God that He would reveal truth to your loved one—truth that he or she needs to refute faulty thinking.

The effectual fervent prayer of a
righteous man availeth much.
—James 5:16 (KJV)

Do not use negative tactics to try to get the person to change or to get his or her attention; it might only make things worse. The negative consequences of a person's OCD manifestations have already gotten his or her attention and bother him or her enough. *The person* wants to change even more than *you* want him or her to change; he or she just may not know how to effect that desired change. When you speak to your loved one, wrap your words with grace. Jesus is the epitome of grace (John 1:17).

Allow your loved one time to heal. Someone who is dealing with OCD is dealing with a health-related issue. OCD affects a person's emotional, psychological, and social well-being. He or she is in need of the Great Physician's touch.

Extend patience to the person who is struggling with OCD. He or she needs love and acceptance—not acceptance that says OCD behavior is healthy but acceptance of the person he or she is and so desperately desires to be. When a person is free to be him- or herself without fear of rejection, this creates an environment conducive to healing. *Patience* is the word of the day. Love is supreme.

Patience and kindness are constant attributes of love. Jealousy, bragging, and arrogance are not part of love's wardrobe; they wouldn't fit her. Love's behavior is appropriate, considerate of others, and shows great restraint. When love is wronged, she continues to be herself—she loves, and even when those who have done her wrong suffer harm, she isn't happy about it. Love treasures truth even when it hurts. No matter how bad it gets, love hangs in there even if it has to be from afar at times. Love believes the best is possible even if things don't look good. She hopes what seems improbable or impossible when others have given up. One of love's greatest qualities is her endurance against all odds. Love is failproof (1 Corinthians 13:4–8).

EPILOGUE

As messed up as I was, God has delivered and continues to deliver me. As bad as this experience has been for me, it is now being used to bless, help, and encourage others. This is what God does. He doesn't allow the enemy's plans against us to win (Genesis 50:20).

Just as the sufferings of Joseph in the book of Genesis had a higher purpose, the sufferings that I have experienced were not in vain. They can't be; otherwise, it would be intolerable to bear. Through that which I have suffered, I am now able to help others with similar situations. I have been abundantly blessed. I have a responsibility to share that which I know with others who may be dealing with similar circumstances so that they, too, may know freedom (Luke 12:48).

The source of comfort is God Himself. No matter what we are going through, no matter the trial, it is the nature of our loving Father's heart to comfort us. God doesn't waste our pain; because we have personally experienced the comfort of God in correlation to that pain, we in turn are able to extend that same comfort to others. They may not be going through the exact same thing as we have, but they could be hurting just as much or more. Whenever we go through a hard time, we are being equipped to help someone else. Likewise, if we have experienced God's comfort, there is someone who needs/will need that same comfort from us (2 Corinthians 1:3–4, 6).

In the Gospel of Luke, there is a story of a city woman who wasn't so good. Upon finding out that Jesus was at a certain person's home, she set out to go there—intently or with trepidation, I do not know—bringing perfume along with her. Her love for Him outweighed any rebuffs or disapproving glances that might come her way. Well aware of what others present might be thinking of her, she was not deterred and positioned herself behind Jesus. Crying tears that held more emotion than words could say, she used those very tears to wet the feet of her Savior. The long hair that cascaded from her head served as the towel to wipe His feet. She poured out her love to Jesus through the kisses she placed upon those most precious feet along with the perfume that she had brought (Luke 7:37–38, 47).

I was and am that woman. I was broken and in disrepair, desperately in need of a Savior. I am that woman, eternally grateful to my heavenly Father for what He has accomplished in my life through His Holy Spirit. Only God knows the depths of my sorrow and the abundance of my joy (Proverbs 14:10).

As much as I have bared my heart and soul through the letters upon these pages, there is more to my story, but it is of a personal nature such that I don't sense a liberty to expound upon it. Although I have shared as much as I have regarding truth that the Holy Spirit has given me, He continues to reveal more and more truth to me resulting in more and more freedom. As the truth upon these pages has been instrumental in opening my door to freedom, I hope and pray that these truths will also help you. This, my story, has been my love letter to you. In the love of Jesus Christ, our Savior and Lord,

—Judith S. Evans

NOTES

1. John 8:32.
2. John 8:32.
3. *The Hebrew-Greek Key Study Bible*, New American Standard, comp. and ed. Spiros Zodhiates, ThD, Lexical Aids to the New Testament.
4. 2 Corinthians 5:21, Romans 10:3–4.
5. *The Hebrew-Greek Key Study Bible*, New American Standard, comp. and ed. Spiros Zodhiates, ThD, Lexical Aids to the New Testament.
6. John 14:17.
7. *The Hebrew-Greek Key Study Bible*, New American Standard, comp. and ed. Spiros Zodhiates, ThD, Lexical Aids to the New Testament, s.v. "5485 Charis."
8. Romans 12:2.
9. 2 Corinthians 10:5.
10. Galatians 5:16–18, 25.
11. 1 Kings 19:12.
12. Romans 12:2.
13. 2 Corinthians 10:5.
14. Galatians 5:16–18, 25.
15. 1 Kings 19:12.

Scripture references taken from *The Hebrew-Greek Key Study Bible*, New American Standard, comp. and ed. by Spiros Zodhiates, ThD, unless otherwise specified.

CPSIA information can be obtained
at www.ICGtesting.com
Printed in the USA
BVHW042153140522
636930BV00002B/135